Richard W Condon was born in Chicago and educated at Suomi College, Hancock, Michigan and the Universities of Nebraska at Omaha and Minnesota. During his graduate work he specialised in Finland during the Second World War, and he is Chairman and Professor of the History Department at Mansfield State College, Mansfield, Pennsylvania

BB

the winter war: Russia against Finland

Richard W Condon

Editor-in-Chief: Barrie Pitt
Editor: David Mason
Art Director: Sarah Kingham
Picture Editor: Robert Hunt
Consultant Art Editor: Denis Piper
Designer: David Penney
Illustration: John Batchelor
Photographic Research: Jonathan Moore
Cartographer: Richard Natkiel

First Printing: October 1972
Printed in United States of America

Ballantine Books Inc.
101 Fifth Avenue New York NY10003

An Intext Publisher

Contents

Victory For Goliath

Introduction by Barrie Pitt

After Russia, America, and Great Britain had become partners in the struggle against Hitler's Germany, it was fashionable in the United States and Britain to regard the Russian leader as an avuncular figure; he was depicted as the benign head of the Soviet worker-state defending itself against Nazi treachery and aggression. Cartoonists made a kindly old gentleman of the heavily-moustached, grim-visaged Stalin, while propagandists suggested a sort of benevolent despot loyally supported by the Russian nation. It was to take considerable experience of Russian cold war tactics during the years following the Second World War before the wartime image of the Soviet dictator was replaced in the West by a more realistic appraisal of his character. Such is the power of the press.

But the Finnish people never suffered from such delusions; to them Stalin was always cast in the same mould as Adolf Hitler, and a considerably more brutal mould than Mussolini, despite the latter's attempt to build a new Roman Empire by employing aircraft and poison gas against Ethiopian tribesmen armed only with rifles. The Finns were aware, when they refused either to hand over

land to the Russians or to allow Soviet bases to be built on their territory, of the risks that they ran, but they saw any concession as a loss of the sovereignty jealously guarded since the signing of the Treaty of Tartu in 1920, whereby the Kremlin officially recognised Finnish independence.

Unfortunately, as part of the Nazi-Soviet Non-Aggression Pact of August 1939 Germany had agreed that Finland should be included in the Soviet sphere of influence, together with Estonia, Latvia, and Lithuania, all of whom – contiguous with Russia and bereft now of the support which German and Russian enmity had previously given them – had no choice but to accede to Russian demands to place military bases on their territory. But the Finns, less accessible from Moscow, and historically more inclined to independence, ignoring the views of both Paasikivi their representative at the Russo-Finnish negotiations, and Field-Marshal Mannerheim their Commander-in-Chief designate, offered only token concessions which were quite unacceptable to Stalin.

A great power, when its importunate injunctions are baulked by a weaker power, rarely resorts immediately to military action. It prefers to look for, or to fabricate, an 'incident' which it can claim as an act of aggression against itself; it then reacts with overwhelming military force. This was the tactic employed by Stalin. Molotov, aggrieved by the stubborn Finnish attitude to the Russian proposals, had earlier set the scene by asking – 'Is it your intention to provoke a conflict?' and on 26th November some Russian soldiers were killed by artillery fire in what was to be known as the Mainila incident; inevitably the Finns were blamed. On 28th November the Soviet government denounced the Russo-Finnish Non-Aggression Pact, and on succeeding days broke off diplomatic relations, and mounted a full-scale attack on Finland.

There could be only one outcome in a war between a nation of 4,000,000 people and a colossus with 180,000,000 inhabitants, and the end came with the Treaty of Moscow signed on 13th March, 1940. But for 105 momentous days from the beginning of December 1939, to the signing of the treaty, a pitifully small Finnish force humbled the mighty Red Army before giving way under sheer weight of numbers.

It was in this campaign that the Russians, traditionally favoured by severe winter weather, found themselves outmatched; it was the Finns, taking every advantage offered by the terrain they knew so well, who glided on skis, white-clad and invisible, to harass and kill the road-bound Russians. Soviet columns were cut up into manageable sections and wiped out one by one; at Suomussulmi the Finns won a classic victory of heroic proportions when two complete Russian divisions were routed by a comparatively small Finnish force.

But in the end, by committing some 1,200,000 men, 1,500 tanks, and 3,000 aircraft to the campaign, the Russians inevitably forced the decision they required. It had taken far longer than expected and was indeed a David and Goliath struggle. Goliath won in the end, for in this battle David had no exceptional weapon to compensate for his relative weakness – but the conflict provided an object lesson in what can be achieved by courage, determination, and good planning. It showed that a small force, using to the full all natural advantages, can inflict damage on an adversary out of all proportion to its military resources.

'Molotov's bread-baskets'

The aftermath of the German liquidation of the Polish state saw the Axis and Allied powers confronting each other but with both sides militarily inactive as the 'phony war' settled over Europe. As the world waited for the next move on the Western Front, events were developing in the far north which were to provide an unexpected diversion from the main theater of operations. There, for 105 days (1st December 1939 to 13th March 1940) an amazed and sympathetic world witnessed a classic struggle as Finland, a nation of 3.5 million people, waged a one-sided war with the Soviet Union's 180 millions. How and why the Winter War came about is as fascinating a story as the battles themselves, combining as it does the Byzantine nature of Kremlin policy, the cynical opportunism of Hitler, and the attempt by the Finns to avoid their assigned role in the German-Soviet division of Eastern Europe.

Finland's assignment to the Soviet sphere of interest by the Molotov-Ribbentrop Agreement of 23rd August 1939, was a role which the Finns were neither consulted about nor prepared to accept. That Finland was expected

Finns inspect a Russian bomber shot down near Viipuri

9

to play buffer for the Soviet Union, however, was not unknown to her people and leaders, for throughout her history she had been cast in that role; indeed, the point had again been under discussion between Helsinki and Moscow since April, 1938. Historical experience and those earlier discussions foreshadowed all the later developments that culminated in the Winter War.

In 1917, when Finland had declared her independence from Russia on 6th December the Finns went to war among themselves to determine whether the new state would be Marxist or Capitalist. After a vicious and brutal civil war in which both the Germans and Bolsheviks participated, the 'Whites', under C G Mannerheim's leadership emerged victorious. With the Treaty of Tartu (Dorpat) in 1920, the independence and sovereignty of Finland had been unequivocally recognized by the Kremlin. The treaty also delineated the frontier between the two states: Finland agreed that Eastern Karelia and the two frontier provinces of Repola and Porajärvi should belong to Russia in order to assure the military defense of Leningrad; in return, the Russians agreed that West Karelia and the ice-free port at Petsamo in the Arctic belonged to Finland; finally, certain Finnish-owned islands in the Gulf of Finland were neutralised. Later, in 1932 and again in 1934, Helsinki and Moscow entered into agreements of non-agression, reaffirming the Treaty of Tartu and establishing a Conciliation Commission 'for amicable settlement . . . of disputes of whatsoever nature'. These agreements were to expire in 1945.

On the basis of these treaties and the policy of neutrality which she

Rudolf Holsti, Finland's Foreign Minister

enunciated, in keeping with the other Scandinavian states, Finland believed herself secure from the machinations of the great powers. Unfortunately, her geopolitical position precluded this. As international tensions increased during the late 1930s, the Soviet Union rapidly emerged from the isolation in which the Revolution and later events had left her and resumed an active role in international affairs. As crisis followed crisis, the importance of Soviet Russia in the international balance of power also grew.

Initially, the Kremlin began to interact with, and put pressure upon, the small states on its western borders. Finland was one of the first to feel the renewed vigor of Russian foreign policy. In April 1938, the Second Secretary of the Soviet Legation in Helsinki, Boris Yartsev, telephoned Foreign Minister Rudolf Holsti for an appointment. Assuming the matter was of some significance, since Yartsev was rumored to be a member of the Soviet Secret Police, Holsti ignored

Above: Ribbentrop and Molotov meet to sign the 1939 agreement which placed Finland within the Russian sphere of influence. *Below:* General Mannerheim in Helsinki during the Finnish civil war.

Left: AK Cajander, Finnish Prime Minister at the time of the Soviet Union's attempt at peaceful expansion in 1938 *Right:* Finnish Minister of Finance Väinö Tanner

diplomatic protocol and agreed to see him. At the meeting on 14th April, Moscow informed the Finnish government that it feared Finland would be a victim of Nazi aggression and her territory used as the northern anchor of a German invasion of the Soviet Union. Holsti was warned that if the Finns did not actively resist such Nazi aggression, the Russians would move to engage the Germans on Finnish territory. Should the Finns resist the Germans, however, Russia was prepared to render all economic and military assistance possible and withdraw the Red Army as soon as the war ended. Yartsev also imposed secrecy upon the whole meeting, to the point of concealing the conversations from the Soviet Minister to Helsinki.

Thus began a series of discussions which lasted for almost a year, eventually bringing Soviet apprehensions and intentions out into the open. From the first, Yartsev talked in vague terms about a Finnish guarantee not to aid Germany in any war against the Soviet Union but repeatedly refused to define his meaning. Even after he began conversations with Prime Minister A K Cajander and Minister of Finance Väinö Tanner, he was no more explicit than he had been with Holsti. He did, however, try to make the Russian proposal more palatable by offering a commercial treaty advantageous to Finland in return for a political agreement directed against Germany.

Since there was no way of learning the exact terms of the Soviet proposal, the discussions dragged on in a desultory fashion during the summer and autumn of 1938. A Finnish draft treaty stated that Finland would continue to adhere to her policy of neutrality and that she would permit no violation of her territory or its use by any great power for an attack upon the Soviet Union, provided she was granted Soviet permission to fortify the Aaland Islands as a safeguard of their neutrality. The Kremlin chose to ignore the draft treaty. A Soviet counter-proposal on 18th August suggested that Finland merely enter into a written understanding that she would resist any German aggression and would call upon Russia for aid if unsuccessful. Russian 'aid' in this case did not necessarily entail the stationing of Red Forces in Finland; rather, Finland was to procure arms from Russia and to sanction the construction of a Soviet airbase on Suursaari (Hogland) in the Gulf of Finland. In return, Russia was prepared to allow Finland to fortify the Aaland Islands with Soviet help, supervision, and partial control and to sign a treaty guaranteeing Finnish territorial integrity and sovereignty; in addition, Russia would enter into a trade agreement favorable to the Finns.

In a full session of the Finnish Government, it was decided to reject the Soviet proposal on the grounds, as Cajander put it, that 'the proposal tends to violate Finland's sovereignty and is in conflict with the policy of neutrality which Finland follows in common with the nations of Scandinavia.' Despite the fact that this was hardly the desired response, the Soviet Union did not pursue the matter at the time. Several months passed in which nothing new was proposed by either side. An attempt to use the dedication of the new Finnish Legation building in Moscow in December as a means to further the negotiations and bring about some sort of agreement proved fruitless, for both sides refused to move from their positions.

In the first months of 1939, there was still no improvement in Russo-Finnish relations; if anything, they deteriorated. The Kremlin refused to enter into a trade agreement until political and military questions were resolved, and the Finns refused to violate their neutrality and sovereignty. In March, Moscow proposed that some of the islands in the Gulf of Finland, neutralized at Soviet insistence in 1920, be leased to the Soviet Union as observation posts. When the Finns declined, it was

Marshal Mannerheim, creator of the much vaunted but mostly obsolete defense lines on the Karelian Isthmus which were named after him

suggested that the islands be ceded to Soviet Russia in exchange for territory in East Karelia north of Lake Ladoga. The Finnish Government turned down this Soviet proposal for several good reasons: firstly, constitutionally, Finnish territory could be ceded only by a five-sixths majority vote in the Diet, but to bring the matter up for debate in that body would obviate the secrecy which had shrouded the discussions at Soviet insistence; secondly, any government making such concessions would commit political suicide; thirdly, if Finland acceded to the Soviet demands, nothing would restrain Germany from making similar demands. As a result of the Finnish response, the discussions were broken off and even the trade negotiations discontinued.

In late April, Germany entered the

13

arena by offering a Non-aggression Pact to the Finns and to the other Scandinavian states. Finland, as well as Sweden and Norway, refused the offer as a violation of neutrality and Scandinavian orientation. To Marshal Mannerheim, however, this Finnish rejection of offers from both great powers in the name of neutrality was

Molotov, with Ribbentrop and Stalin looking on, signs the Nazi-Soviet non-aggression pact in Moscow

unrealistic, since it only served to worsen relations with both while doing nothing to increase the security of Finland.

Whatever the case, the Finnish Government continued to pursue its precarious policy of neutrality in a steadily worsening international atmosphere. First came the Austrian *Anschluss* and then the Munich meeting to dismember Czechoslovakia in 1938, a meeting to which Russia, an ally of the Czechs, was not invited.

With the subsequent German occupation of that state and of the Memel District, however, Russia suddenly emerged as the key to maintaining the international balance. Already suspicious of Finland, the Soviet Union began capitalizing upon her new status to secure an agreement with Britain and France or Germany which would recognize the Baltic states and Finland as being within the Soviet sphere of influence.

In March, the British and the French initiated negotiations with the Soviet Government which were designed to contain Germany. These negotiations were seized upon by the Kremlin leaders as a golden opportunity to get Western recognition of their right to guarantee aid to the Baltic states and Finland in the event of an attack upon them. To be included in such an agreement was the provision of aid in the case of 'indirect aggression', i.e. the assumption of a pro-German attitude on the part of any government so guaranteed.

When rumors of this provision surfaced, a chill of apprehension passed through Finland. Supported by Sweden, the Finnish Government made strong protests in London and Paris and succeeded in getting the Allies to declare that any proposal which included Finland was unacceptable. For this and other reasons, the Anglo-Franco-Russian discussions, which continued into the summer, were doomed to failure.

Meanwhile, in April, the Russians initiated trade negotiations with Germany which soon moved into the political sphere. Unencumbered by moral and juridical sensibilities, the *Reich* government had no qualms about allocating some of its neighbors to the Soviet sphere of influence, including Finland. As far as Berlin was concerned, at the moment there was no Nazi-Soviet conflict of interests in the Baltic region. So, on 23rd August, Joachim von Ribbentrop flew to Moscow to conclude a Non-aggression Pact with Molotov. At the cere-

Elias Erkko, called to Moscow to discuss the Russian demands on Finland

monies, a new era in Nazi-Soviet relations was proclaimed. Despite stout denials by both Germany and the Soviet Union, Finland had been included in the Soviet sphere of influence. She was soon to discover the exact import of this demarcation.

How Hitler used the Ribbentrop-Molotov Pact to shield his invasion of Poland on 1st September and how the Soviet Union, after first announcing her neutrality, hurled herself upon the prostrate Poles on the 17th, on the grounds that the war had revealed the 'internal bankruptcy of the Polish state', are well-known. This fourth partition of Poland prepared the way for complete Soviet domination of the Baltic states and of Finland. First Estonia on 28th September, then Latvia on 5th October and Lithuania on the 11th had fallen into line and acceded to Soviet demands for military bases on their territory. Meanwhile, Finland's turn came on the 5th when Molotov requested Finnish Foreign Minister Elias Erkko to journey to Moscow to discuss 'certain concrete questions of a political nature'. When, by the 8th, the Finnish Government had not replied, Derevyanski called on Erkko to impress upon him the need for haste, pointing out that Finland was not treating the matter as the other Baltic states had. Erkko retorted: 'I have no knowledge as to how the Baltic States were invited to Moscow; Finland has dealt with the matter as a normal affair and in the normal course.' Obviously, Finland was not about to capitulate to Soviet pressure.

It was decided that J K Paasikivi, Finnish envoy to Stockholm, should head the Finnish delegation to Moscow, since it was felt that Erkko's place was with the government. Assuming that the Kremlin's 'concrete questions' would center on the earlier discussions and the sort of demands recently agreed to by the Baltic states, the Finnish Government instructed Paasikivi to emphasize that Finland's policy of neutrality, her small size, and the Treaty of Tartu and the Non-aggression Pact with the USSR militated against her becoming a threat to the Soviet Union. Any territorial concessions were to be ruled out, as was the establishment of Soviet military bases on the Finnish mainland, or on the Aaland Islands and any territorial adjustments on the Karelian Isthmus. Only under extreme pressure was Paasikivi to concede some small islands in the Gulf of Finland, but not Suursaari. Any concessions were to be reciprocal, and the compensation would have to appear reasonable to the world. Finally, no discussion of a mutual assistance treaty was permitted.

Thus instructed, the Finnish delegation departed for Moscow on 9th October and began negotiations on the 12th. Finland's worst fears were quickly realized in the first session. Stalin demanded everything Paasikivi was forbidden to discuss: a mutual assistance treaty, the lease of a naval base for stationing 5,000 troops on Hanko Cape at the mouth of the Gulf of Finland, the western part of the Fisherman's Peninsula on the Arctic Ocean, the removal of the Finno-Soviet border on the Karelian Isthmus some twelve kilometres westward (dangerously close to Viipuri, Finland's second largest city), and some islands in the Gulf of Finland, including Suursaari. In all, Stalin wanted 2,761 square kilometres of developed Finnish territory in exchange for 5,529 square kilometres of undeveloped

Ancient cannon on Hanko Cape whose possession by Finland was considered by Russia a threat to Leningrad

land north of Lake Ladoga. He also suggested the demolition of fortifications on both sides of the frontier because they were 'prejudicial to peaceful relations'.

Unprepared for the magnitude of the Soviet demands, Paasikivi returned to Helsinki for new instructions. There, the government concluded that under no circumstances could Hanko be leased to the USSR; on the other hand, five small islands could be ceded for compensation, a small westward adjustment of the Karelian border could be accepted, and the 1932 Non-aggression Pact could be redrafted to state that neither party would aid another state attacking one of the contracting powers. If it became necessary, Paasikivi was also authorized to cede the southern part of Suursaari and, if pressed, the whole island, to keep Hanko out of jeopardy. With regard to the Fisherman's Peninsula, there was to be no yielding.

Unwilling to conduct the negotiations without a member of the government present, Paasikivi was accompanied by Tanner on his return

to Moscow. When the new proposals were presented to Stalin on the 23rd, he declared them inadequate, insisting that the Soviet demands were minimal and could not be reduced by bargaining. After some two hours of futile discussions, the session ended in a curt exchange between Molotov and Paasikivi. Molotov asked, 'Is it your intention to provoke a conflict?' Paasikivi shot back, 'We want no such thing, but you seem to'.

On that note the discussion ended, and Paasikivi and Tanner prepared to return to Helsinki. But a few hours later Molotov's secretary appeared at the Finnish Legation to request their presence for another parley. When they arrived at the Kremlin, Stalin began as though there had been no break in the discussions. He offered to reduce the number of troops on Hanko to 4,000, to decrease the territorial demands on the Karelian Isthmus, and to accept the Finnish proposal for the expansion of the Non-aggression Pact. Although the

latter was acceptable, the first two remained more than the Finns were willing to concede: even 4,000 troops at Hanko laid Finland's heavily populated industrial heartland open to attack from within and the shift in the border would still place it dangerously near Viipuri. Unable to commit their government to these proposals, Paasikivi and Tanner returned to Helsinki for consultations. At the same time Tanner addressed an inquiry to the Swedish Government asking whether Finland could expect its support in the event of war. On the 27th, the Swedish Prime Minister Hansson replied that Sweden would continue to supply Finland with arms, munitions, equipment, food, and diplomatic support, but nothing more was to be expected for fear of German reprisals.

Thus, virtually left to their own devices, the Finns moved into the final phase of the negotiations. After intensive discussion in the cabinet and with the party leaders in the Diet,

18

a firm stand was taken against Stalin's proposals. No base was to be leased at Hanko, but the border might be moved somewhat westwards on the Isthmus (but far short of Stalin's demands), the western part of the Fisherman's Peninsula could be ceded, and the small islands in the Gulf of Finland were again offered. Stalin's suggestion that the fortifications on both sides of the Karelian frontier be demolished was also refused on the grounds that Finland's fortifications were required only for defense and for the preservation of Finnish neutrality.

En route to Moscow, Paasikivi and Tanner received word that Molotov had announced the full details of the negotiations in his speech to the Supreme Soviet on 31st October. Uncertain of what this publicity

Swedish Prime Minister Hansson. He offered Finland diplomatic and material aid but no troops for fear of German reprisals

JK Paasikivi and Tanner en route to Moscow in an attempt to negotiate with Stalin

portended, the Finns nevertheless decided to press on to Moscow in the hopes that there would still be room for negotiations. Their qualified optimism proved unfounded, for the Finnish proposals were declared inadequate almost before they were fully presented, and no further compromises were forthcoming from Stalin. Before leaving the Kremlin, Molotov remarked, 'We civilians can see no further in the matter; now it is the turn of the military to have their say.' On this ominous note the Finns departed for home.

Throughout November matters were relatively calm in spite of a steady stream of invective against Finland in the Soviet press and repeated violations of Finnish airspace by Soviet aircraft. Nonetheless, an optimistic belief prevailed in the Finnish Government that a bad phase had passed and affairs with Russia would improve. This feeling was strengthened by a report on the 23rd that the American Ambassador to Moscow did not believe the USSR would attack

Finland.

Three days later the Finns' illusions were shattered by the Mainila incident. In a note from Molotov, the Finns were accused of directing artillery fire at the village of Mainila on the Karelian Isthmus, killing four men and wounding nine others. The note pointed out that the Finns had been warned about the danger of concentrating troops on the border and that this incident was a conse-quence of Finnish refusal to withdraw them. Molotov proposed that Finnish troops be withdrawn some twenty-five kilometres from the frontier to 'preclude all possibility of a repetition of provocative acts.'

From this point, relations rapidly deteriorated between the two states. Helsinki denied the charges and suggested that Soviet troops had accidentally fired upon the village, since three Finnish border guards had

reported artillery fire from the south of Mainila on that day. Indeed, the Finns could hardly have been responsible since Mannerheim had ordered all artillery removed from within range of the frontier in mid-October to obviate just such a possibility. The Finns did, however, declare their willingness to negotiate a mutual withdrawal of troops from the border and also suggested a joint inquiry into the incident.

On the 28th, Molotov rejected the Finnish proposals, accusing the Finnish Government of harboring 'deep hostility' towards the USSR. Furthermore, to withdraw Soviet troops the suggested distance from the border would be to place them in the suburbs of Leningrad, 'which would be absurd'. The Finnish refusal to withdraw unilaterally was viewed as a deliberate decision to keep Leningrad under a direct threat by Finnish troops. Such reasoning led the Soviet Government to conclude that Finland no longer abided by the Non-aggression Pact; Molotov accordingly announced the Soviet Union's unilateral renunciation of the pact.

Without bothering to await a Finnish reply to this note, the Kremlin severed diplomatic relations with Finland on 29th November. Still bending every effort to avoid war, the Finns nevertheless sent a conciliatory reply to the previous day's note and reiterated their suggestion for a joint investigation with a view to a peaceful settlement of the dispute. The Finns also agreed to withdraw all but units of frontier guards and customs officials to such a distance from Leningrad as to no longer constitute a threat to the city. During the day, however, a Red force crossed the frontier at Petsamo and took several Finnish border guards prisoner. The full Soviet answer to the Finnish note came on the 30th in an all-out attack upon Finland by land, sea, and air.

That morning, Russian bombers out of Estonia dived low over Helsinki and other cities to unload their cargoes of bombs. According to the Soviet radio, the Finnish reports of these air raids were fabrications, for the Russian Air Force had merely dropped bread to the starving masses of Helsinki. Thereafter, the Finns referred to Soviet bombs as 'Molotov's bread-baskets'. Humor aside, Finland was in a fight for her very life.

Tanner suggests a mutual withdrawal of Soviet and Finnish forces from the border

21

'Molotov's bread-baskets' fall on
Helsinki 30th November 1939

The cold facts

No one, least of all the Finns, believed Finland could withstand the Soviet onslaught for any length of time. Her only aim was to hold the invader at bay in the hope that outside help would arrive before a catastrophe occurred or, barring the latter, to make any attack so costly as to cause the aggressor to agree to some sort of peaceful settlement.

Since independence, it had been commonly accepted among Finnish military leaders that the only potential aggressor was Russia. Hence, the Finns were prepared psychologically and defensively to deal with the threat from the East. The driving force behind these preparations throughout the period between the two world wars had been Marshal Mannerheim. Although in retirement during the 'twenties, he had maintained an active interest in the defensive preparedness of his country, sending promising young officers to study in German and French military schools while constantly urging defensive measures on the eastern frontier. When he assumed the chairmanship of the National Defense Council in 1931, he undertook to accomplish his objectives with characteristic energy and thoroughness.

Military service had been compulsory since 1922, with provisions for seven years' active reserve service (Defense Corps) and twenty-four years'

Russian bombers visit a Finnish town

**Finnish army maneuvers at Karelia
just before the outbreak of war**

inactive reserve status after a one-year tour of duty. The Defense Corps had been organized on a cadre system whereby it could be called up and integrated into the regular units to double their size. Mannerheim recognized the dangers inherent in the inefficiency and slowness of this mobilization system, since it would require two weeks for the reserves to reach the frontier, more time would be consumed in assimilating the new forces into the regular units, and the procedure would concentrate men, materials, weapons, and supplies in a few locations, making them susceptible to air attacks. Consequently, the Defense Corps was reorganized on a territorial basis, so that complete units could be despatched to the front after the assignment of regular officers

Hurried attempts are made in the summer of 1939 to strengthen the Mannerheim Line

to the territorial organizations. In this fashion the field army could be quickly reinforced before the invader was able to make any deep penetrations through the frontier of defenses, the nation's resources could be more fully marshalled, and either partial or complete mobilization would be permitted, as the exigencies of the moment required.

Throughout the 1930s Mannerheim unceasingly urged the Diet to appropriate larger funds to the defense budget. Because of the world-wide financial crisis in the early 'thirties, his arguments went mostly unheeded. Nevertheless, measures to strengthen the defenses on the Karelian Isthmus – the gateway for any invasion – to acquire supplies and armaments, and to train the armed forces were undertaken with energy and with intelligent utilization of the resources available. During 1931 and 1932 some 100,000 unemployed were set to work

Finnish reservists march towards Johannes during mobilization

on the Isthmus, constructing concrete machine gun nests and trenches and anti-tank traps of stones and concrete. During the summer and fall of 1939, further defensive fortifications of the same sort were built there by a volunteer labor force of students and other concerned citizens.

Perhaps the most serious handicap to Mannerheim's efforts was the failure to procure adequate allocations for capital expenditures for material replacements. The budget was cut by ten per cent for 1932 and again for 1933. As a result, the expansion of the cartridge factory was deferred indefinitely, and the extra money requested for implementing the territorial system was drawn from that allocated for material replacements. By the late 'thirties, matters had improved somewhat, and the Diet began to attend the needs of the military as the international scene grew more bleak. In Mannerheim's opinion, however, too little was done early enough to stave off a disaster in the event of war. And, in a sense, he was right, for if the money required for the defense needs of the country had been forthcoming, Fin-

land would have been in a far better position to deal with the Soviet threat in 1939 than she actually was.

The Finns thus found themselves at war with the cartridge factory still incomplete, the defense of the Karelian Isthmus inadequate and largely obsolete despite the efforts put forth in 1939, with an air force consisting mostly of antiquated planes, and a regular army of only 33,000 officers and men. Upon mobilization, thanks to the territorial system, this force could be increased to nine divisions, or 127,800 men, including supporting troops. In addition, there were about 100,000 army reservists who could be called up and another 100,000 men in the Civic Guard who drilled and maneuvered at regular intervals with the regular army and could be integrated into it. All told, Finland could raise about 400,000 men in the army, Civic Guard, navy and coast guard. Finally, there was the 100,000-strong *Lovta Svärd*, the women's auxiliary to the Civic Guard, made up of trained cooks, military clerks, laundry

Part of the 100,000-strong Civic Guard capable of immediate integration with the regular army

workers, and nurses, who thus freed almost all the manpower for service on the front.

But the country was still inadequately prepared for the ordeal ahead, as a comparison of Finnish and Soviet forces indicates. In 1939, the following facts were known: a Finnish division consisted of 14,200 men as compared to 17,500 for the Russians; a Soviet division contained two artillery regiments, whose fire power was three times that of the one Finnish artillery regiment per division; the Russians had an anti-tank section, an armored battalion with forty to fifty tanks, and an AA company with each division, whereas a Finnish division possessed none of these complements; finally, in automatic weapons and grenade launchers, a Soviet division was twice as strong as its Finnish counterpart. In addition, there were a number of armored and reserve artillery units under the immediate command of the Soviet Commander-in-Chief, the Soviet forces had a virtually unlimited supply of munitions, they commanded the air with approximately 800 aircraft at the outbreak of hostilities in comparison to Finland's ninety-six, and they had absolute material and industrial superiority.

Finland was further handicapped by the inadequacy of her war materials. According to Mannerheim, under war conditions the Finns had the following: two months' supply of cartridges for rifles, automatic weapons, machine guns, fuel and lubricating oils; one month's supply of aviation fuel; twenty-four days' supply of 122mm howitzer shells; twenty-two days' supply of 81mm grenade projectiles; enough 77mm field gun shells to last twenty-one days; and nineteen days' supply of heavy artillery shells. These deficiencies were to be partially rectified by purchases and shipments from Sweden and other states but at no time was Finland anywhere near equality with her foe. To these figures must be added the fact that, just prior

Lovta Stard (Finnish Women's Auxiliary Army) members whose services released much-needed manpower for the front

to the attack, the Finns had only 100 anti-tank weapons, half of which were supplied by Sweden and the other half by home industry ,and only a few batteries of AA guns and heavy artillery.

Neither were the disparities between the opposing forces compensated for by Finnish frontier fortifications. Such fortifications as existed were quite modest, many were hastily constructed, and most were obsolete. The impregnability of the so-called 'Mannerheim Line' (eighty-eight miles of fortifications on the Karelian Isthmus) was a myth propagated by Soviet propaganda to rationalize the incompetency and failures of the massive Russian attempt to invade Finland. It never approached anything like the 'Maginot' or 'Siegfried' Lines in depth or in fortifications.

Barbed wire entanglements on the Mannerheim Line were to prove totally inadequate against Russian armor

In reality, of the sixty-six machine gun nests on the Line, forty-four dated from the twenties and were faultily constructed and located. The other twenty-two were of more recent construction but unable to withstand heavy fire, as the war proved. In addition, there were some tank traps and barbed-wire entanglements, neither of which proved very effective against tank attacks. As Mannerheim said himself 'The Mannerheim Line is the Finnish soldier standing in the snow.'

Because they lacked adequate materials, weapons, and supplies for complete mobilization, the Finns were unable to field their fifteen divisions by calling up the reserves. In early autumn eight complete divisions were mobilized, and by the end of October there were nine, as a result of combining the covering troops on the Karelian Isthmus into one division. At the outbreak of hostilities these nine divisions were deployed as follows: the Army of the

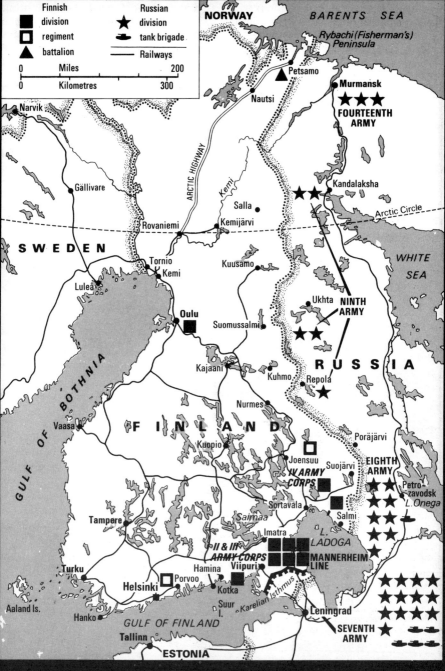

Finnish
- ■ division
- □ regiment
- ▲ battalion

Russian
- ★ division
- tank brigade
- Railways

Miles 0 — 200
Kilometres 0 — 300

NORWAY

BARENTS SEA

Rybachi (Fisherman's) Peninsula

Petsamo ▲

Nautsi

Murmansk
★ ★ ★
FOURTEENTH ARMY

Kemi
ARCTIC HIGHWAY

Gällivare

Salla

Kandalaksha
★ ★

Arctic Circle

Rovaniemi
Kemijärvi

SWEDEN

Kuusamo

WHITE SEA

Tornio
Kemi

Luleå

Oulu ■

Suomussalmi

Ukhta
NINTH ARMY
★ ★

RUSSIA

Kajaani

Kuhmo

Repola
★

Nurmes

FINLAND

Vaasa

Kuopio

Poräjärvi

GULF OF BOTHNIA

Joensuu □

Suojärvi

EIGHTH ARMY
★ ★

IV ARMY CORPS ■

Petro-zavodsk
L. Onega
★ ★

Sortavala

Salmi
★

Tampere

Saimaa

Imatra

L. LADOGA
★ ★ ★ ★

II & III ARMY CORPS ■ ■ ■
■ ■ ■

MANNERHEIM LINE

Turku

Hamina
Viipuri ■

★ ★ ★ ★

Helsinki
Porvoo □

Kotka
Suur I.

Karelian Isthmus

★ ★ ★ ★

Aaland Is.

Hanko

GULF OF FINLAND

Leningrad

SEVENTH ARMY
★

Tallinn

ESTONIA

Karelian Isthmus (six divisions) was divided into II and III Army Corps; the reserve of the Commander-in-Chief (6th Division) was held in the vicinity west of Viipuri, engaged in preparing fortifications and on the alert for a hostile landing between Viipuri and Kotka; IV Army Corps of two divisions held the sixty-mile front north of Lake Ladoga to Suojärvi. An additional general reserve division (the 9th) was assembling at Oulu, while only independent companies and battalions, mostly Civic

Secret road building before hostilities allowed the Russians to deploy far more troops than the Finns expected

Guard units, defended the remaining 625-mile front from Suojärvi to the Arctic Ocean. Later, these units became the nucleus of the operative groups which were organized during the war.

Finland's nine divisions faced an initial Soviet attacking force of five armies comprising thirty divisions and six tank brigades. The main Russian force, the Seventh Army (later divided into the Seventh and Thirteenth Armies), consisted of thirteen divisions which were launched against the Karelian Isthmus; however, only seven divisions participated in the first offensives. In support of this army were five tank brigades

and several regiments of heavy artillery. The objective of its left wing was to occupy Viipuri and advance from there into the heartland of Finland, while the right wing took the Kemi-Sortavla-Leningrad railroad. According to Mannerheim, the number of troops deployed on the Isthmus surprised the Finns: it had been assumed that the enemy would be unable to utilize effectively more than three divisions because of the terrain and the lack of roads in the area, both of which would make a nightmare of logistics. The size of the invasion, however, made it clear that the Russian attack had long been planned, especially when it was learned that the Russians had built roads up to the frontier and stockpiled large amounts of supplies and munitions on their side of the border.

North of Lake Ladoga the Soviet Eighth Army of nine divisions, a tank brigade, and heavy artillery was to advance south around the lake and take the Finnish forces on the Isthmus from the rear, also penetrating to the railroad. Further north, the Ninth Army, consisting of five divisions, was responsible for cutting Finland at the waist by a drive from the area of Kandalaksh-Uhtua-Repola to the northern end of the Gulf of Bothnia and for severing connections with Sweden. In the Arctic, Four-

eenth Army (three divisions) had as
ts objective the port of Petsamo and
, southward advance from there
long the Arctic Highway. The latter
wo armies had no independent tank
rigades but were supported by forty
r fifty tanks for each division.

Thus, faced by the cold facts of the
verwhelming superiority of their
dversary, the Finns went into battle
ith slim hopes of holding the line
ntil help arrived. Not surprisingly,
ittle or no material help was forth-
oming from the rest of the world,
lthough a torrent of rhetoric and
ympathy filled the halls of the League
f Nations, the world press, and most

Foreign Office news releases. Both
Sweden and the United States offered
to mediate a peace settlement, but
the Soviet Government rejected the
overture.

Meanwhile, the Finnish Government was reorganized, with Risto Ryti
as Prime Minister and Väinö Tanner
as Foreign Minister. It was hoped that
this reorganization would lead the
Kremlin to reopen negotiations and
settle the conflict peacefully since the
former government was discredited
as obstructionist in Stalin's eyes.
These hopes were soon dashed. On 3rd
December the new government ap-
pealed to the League of Nations, but

American and Swedish volunteers

was a Kremlin puppet government headed by the exiled Finnish Communist, Otto Kuusinen, and located in the border hamlet of Terijoki, which had fallen to the Russians on the first day of war.

Undeceived by Molotov's cunning the League condemned the Soviet actions and expelled her from the organization. Member and non-member states were urged to render Finland every humanitarian and material assistance possible. This was the League's last practical achievement and it was perhaps a fitting swan song. Further efforts by the Finnish government to make contact with the Kremlin proved fruitless. On 15th December Tanner made a radio appeal to Molotov to reopen the negotiations. The only response was a laconic statement by the Tass agency that the appeal was unlikely to receive a reply.

In response to the League's call assistance from other states was mainly diplomatic, although some material aid was rendered. Sweden supplied the most substantial aid since large quantities could be transported to Finland with ease. This aid was of inestimable value and decisive importance to Finland because of her dire lack of arms and munitions. Volunteers also came from Sweden but only two battalions saw action; some also came from Britain, the United States, Hungary, and elsewhere. None of the latter saw any action except a group of Finnish Americans who reached the front a few days before the end of hostilities. Of greater importance was an American loan of $30,000,000 which, unfortunately, was limited to civilian purchases and was not approved by Congress until February of the following year. Given the conditions of the time, however, the lack of concrete aid was probably to be expected, since all nations were rearming and needed everything for their own defense.

the Russians refused to attend the sessions dealing with the war. Molotov gave as the reason that 'the USSR is not at war with Finland and does not threaten the Finnish nation with war.' He went on to say the Soviet Union 'maintains peaceful relations with the Democratic Republic of Finland, whose Government signed with the USSR on 2nd December [a] Pact of Mutual Assistance and Friendship. This Pact settles all questions which the Soviet Government had fruitlessly discussed with the delegates [of the] former Finnish Government now divested of its power.' The 'Democratic Republic of Finland' referred to

The first round

Just what the Russian plan of ground operations was in the first stages of the war is a matter of disagreement among writers and military analysts, and the Russians have always remained secretive about it. Their disposition of troops does not provide evidence of a major effort at any one point, despite the relatively large concentration on the Karelian Isthmus. This concentration was, in fact, only natural since the Isthmus was the traditional gateway of invasion into the Finnish heartland and because the major Finnish defensive efforts were undertaken there. In all likelihood, the Russians did not believe that any point was more important than another for a breakthrough, since they were apparently convinced that Finland would collapse at the first shot, aided, of course, by fifth columnists inside Finland. Consequently, during December they did little in the way of making concentrated and coordinated efforts at any one point.

Taking a page from Russian tactics against Napoleon, the Finns destroyed every building and road as they withdrew from the frontier. This 'scorched earth' policy left the Russians massed

Russian guns open fire against the Finnish positions

The Finns' planned withdrawal to the Karelian Isthmus lines caused heavy casualties to the pursuing Soviets

on bad roads, and without any shelter from the sub-zero weather. Thus, as the enemy met with staunch resistance and as his advance was stopped, he was left in the unenviable situation of not only having to camp out but also of being constantly harassed around his campfires at night by Finnish ski patrols. The easy victory envisioned by the Soviet planners was not to be.

Russian lack of coordination and concentration in attacking also permitted the Finns to delay the invaders on the greater length of the frontier with only limited personnel and weapons by utilizing the natural defenses of the terrain; thus, they were able to concentrate the bulk of their forces on the Karelian Isthmus. Mobilization in the fall had deployed the field army at staging areas, from which it could move quickly to support the covering troops.

Delaying tactics had been standard in Finnish planning since independence, especially on the Isthmus, where the aggressor was to be admitted into a defensive zone twelve to thirty miles deep while the Finns inflicted the heaviest possible losses upon him. This defensive zone was ideal for the purpose: long, narrow lakes and swamps, still unfrozen, and

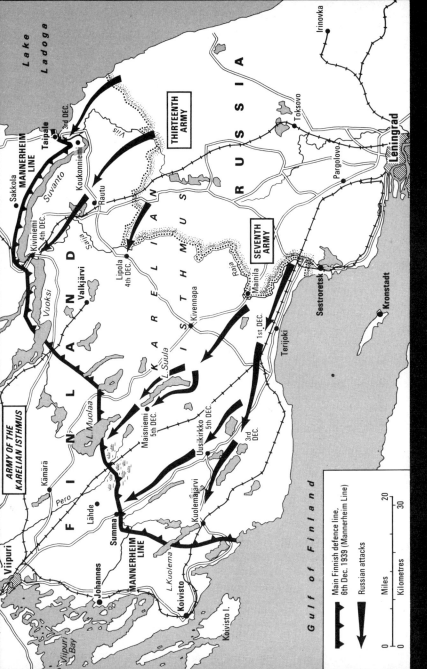

The Russian advance to the Mannerheim Line

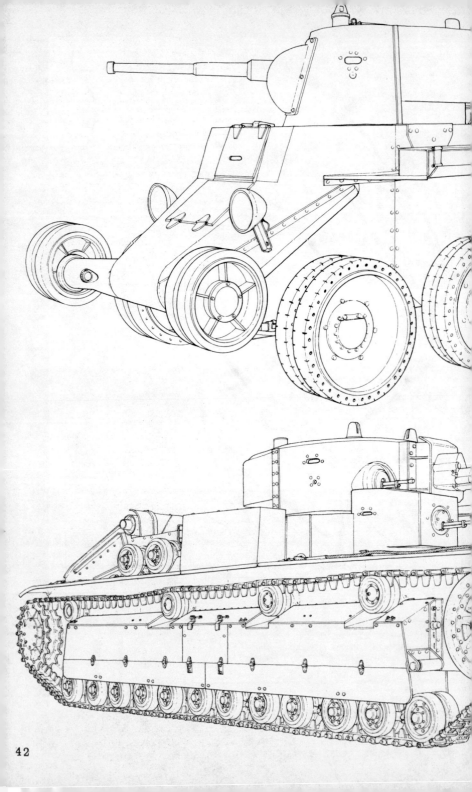

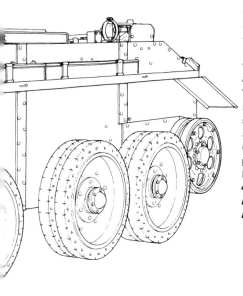

The Soviet BT-7-2 light tank. This tank, introduced in 1935, had Christie-type suspension in which the tracks could be removed for high speed road travel. It was an excellent tank for its time, and gave the Russians the experience on which to base the T-34 and their large-scale tank tactics. *Weight :* 13.8 tons. *Crew :* three. *Armament :* one 45mm gun with 188 rounds and two 7.62mm machine guns with 2,394 rounds. *Armour :* 15mm turret front, sides and rear ; 13mm hull front, side and rear, and floor ; 10mm turret roof ; 6-10mm hull roof ; and 22mm glacis plate. *Engine :* one M-17T modified Liberty aero engine, 450-hp. *Speed :* 45mph maximum. *Range :* 310 maximum. *Length :* 18.65 feet. *Width :* 7.89 feet. *Height :* 6.33 feet.

The Russian T28M medium tank. The T28 series first appeared in 1933, and mounted a 76.2mm howitzer as main armament. Later, the T28B appeared, mounting a 76.2mm gun in place of the howitzer to enable it to fight in tank against tank battles. Later again, it was up-armoured, from 30mm to 80mm, and it was this version, the T28M, which the Russians used in the Russo-Finnish War. The last variant was not successful, however, as the added weight of the new armour made the tank very slow and lacking in agility. *Weight :* about 33 tons (the basic T28 weighed 27.5 tons). *Crew :* 6. *Armament :* one 76.2mm gun with 70 rounds and four 7.62mm machine guns with 7,938 rounds. *Armour :* 80mm maximum, 20mm minimum. *Speed :* 18mph. *Radius of action :* 90 miles. *Power :* M17 12-cylinder engine, 500hp at 1450rpm. *Length :* 24 feet 9 inches. *Height :* 9 feet 4 inches. *Width :* 9 feet 4 inches.

heavy forests restricted the movements of the enemy to narrow passages where he could not maneuver and could be easily and unobservedly outflanked. While the area was unknown to the Russians, for the Finnish troops it was almost as well-known as their own backyards, because they had practiced maneuvers there during the summer. At ease in these wilds and unencumbered by heavy equipment and machinery, the Finnish soldiers moved quickly, silently, and effectively on their skis against the invaders.

As is often the case, however, all did not go as planned in the war room. Against explicit orders from Mannerheim, the insufficient and inadequately armed covering troops often engaged in direct combat with the Russians without proper support from the field army, thus making long delaying actions impossible. Direct combat proved ineffective because the Russians advanced, as expected, in long columns along narrow roads congested by their own convoys and covered by tanks. Because of their inadequate forces and artillery, the Finnish troops were unable to assail the enemy as effectively as they could otherwise have done However, had there been close coordination between the cover troops and the field army, the invaders could have been dealt more severe blows in spite of the Finns' deficiencies.

Nevertheless, the Russian advance was delayed and by 2nd December the invaders had only reached the first Finnish defense lines, some six to ten miles inside the Finnish frontier.

Finnish columns during the withdrawal to the Mannerheim Line

Minor breakthroughs occurred, but these were soon rectified by sharp counterattacks the following night and the line was stabilized. Some important territory was lost due to a curious and unexplained incident late in the evening of the 2nd. A report reached the Finnish Army Staff at Imatra that Red forces had landed on the coast behind the covering troops, while another force was supposed to have penetrated the Finnish center right up to the main defense line. Before learning that the report was false, the right wing of the covering troops was withdrawn to a new position at Uusikirkko and the left wing was withdrawn beyond the west bank of the Suvanto River, past the defensive line of II Army Corps. Unfortunately, the withdrawal took place so fast that orders to retake the territory could not be fulfilled. Thus, the Russians gained some valuable ground without firing a shot.

This incident revealed that even among the covering troops coordination was bad. This can be explained, in part, by the Finns' inadequate communications: they did not possess any up to date equipment, and what they had frequently failed to function properly. In any case, the withdrawal of the wings of the Finnish forces, caused by the false report of a Russian breakthrough, produced a situation in which part of the troops on the eastern end of the Isthmus were pulled back while one group of II Army Corps was left exposed near Lipola. The situation was not rectified until two days later.

On the 4th a threatened enemy attack upon the Uusikirkko sector resulted in a crisis of major proportions. Again, the lack of coordination caused a grave loss of time in the delaying actions necessary for the field army to arrive at its positions. In this case, a Red armored brigade and its infantry units advanced around the south end of Lake Suula, quickly penetrating the weak positions held by the exhausted Finns.

Lieutenant-General H Öhquist, Finnish commander on the east side of the Isthmus

The covering troops in front of Uusikirkko retreated to the north of the village, expecting a Russian advance in that direction. Instead, the enemy turned its main thrust northward on the west side of the lake toward Maisniemi, moving parallel to its weaker wing, which proceeded up the east shore, thus threatening to trap the covering troops holding the area between Lakes Suula and Muolaa in a pincer.

At the same time, the Finnish troops at Lipola were hard pressed and had to evacuate their position for a new one further north. It is amazing that they had held out in their exposed position for so long without any reinforcements. In fact, two divisions, the 1st and the 11th, had been designated by Mannnerheim's Headquarters on 1st December as relief forces for the east side of the Isthmus, but the commander of the sector, Lieutenant-General Öhquist felt that he needed them elsewhere. In the event, the 1st

Kiviniemi, scene of one of the Russian penetrations of the Finns' defenses

and 11th Divisions were not used to reinforce any sector; this development brought Mannerheim to Imatra on the 3rd to deliver a personal reprimand to the commanders for being too passive at critical moments of the crisis.

On the morning of the 4th, the Russians attacked and took the bridgehead at Kiviniemi. The following day, they again attacked the area around Uusikirkko and also broke through the defenses at Maisniemi, thus threatening the 5th Division with encirclement. The tank attack at Maisniemi precipitated such a panic that weapons, equipment, and field kitchens were forgotten in the rush to get away. A cavalry troop with the forces was especially terrified, causing a soldier to ask the next day: 'Is there really in existence a worse combination than panicked men on the backs of panicked horses?'

This was not the only time the Finns were panicked by armored attacks in those first confusing days of the war. But their terror is understandable when one considers that most of them had never seen more than one or two tanks at any one time, while here they were facing them in large numbers and with scarcely any anti-tank guns.

To compensate for the lack of such weapons, detachments supplied with mines were formed in every company during the first weeks of the war. Finnish ingenuity, however, soon asserted itself and brought forth a simpler, but more effective anti-tank weapon, the 'Molotov cocktail'. Simplicity itself, the device consisted of a bottle filled with potassium chloride, kerosene, with novlen and an ampoule of sulphuric acid attached to the mouth of the bottle to detonate it. The means of delivery was a daredevil on skis, who slipped alongside a Soviet tank and threw the cocktail into the turret.

During the last stages of the delaying actions, closer cooperation between the various covering groups was realized, and they accordingly dealt the Russians some heavy blows. Only a couple of minor breakthroughs in the main defense line occurred during the delaying operations. Both

Covering troops withdraw from Suvilahti on the third day of the Winter War

were in the eastern sector of the Isthmus: one at Koukonniemi on the 6th, with cost heavy to the Russians, and the second at Kiviniemi on the 7th.

By the 6th the primary task of the covering troops was complete, and they were withdrawn to the main positions. For the moment the situation on the Isthmus was stabilized. Along the whole 800-mile front, the Finnish covering troops of approximately 13,000 men had held the Russians up, except at Petsamo, although they faced approximately 140,000 troops and some 1,000 tanks. Wherever the Finns had given way, Russian armor had played a decisive role. Finnish anti-tank guns were effective, as proved by the eighty tanks destroyed before 5th December, but they were too heavy and cumbersome for the rapid movements demanded by mobile warfare. It was in these situations that the 'Molotov cocktail' was to prove its worth.

There is no doubt that events had taken an unexpected turn from the viewpoint of the Soviet strategists. The Soviet press had trumpeted that Finland would collapse in a few days, and apparently the military leaders

believed their own propaganda, for a Soviet order captured during the first days of battle warned the Soviet troops not to violate the Swedish frontier.

Poorly prepared to face a determined adversary and forced to fight in the narrow corridors between the lakes and forests on roads badly damaged by the retreating Finns and congested by their own troops, the Soviet troops came to a grinding halt. Instead of a *blitzkrieg*, it had taken them a week just to reach the Finnish main defense line. This was certainly not going to be another Poland.

Not only were the Russians halted on the Karelian Isthmus, but their other efforts were as singularly unsuccessful. Obviously, the Kuusinen government at Terikoji, if it ever really set itself up there, was to be the main thrust of a fifth column attack. However, Kuusinen's appeals to the Finnish working class to rise up against its oppressors either fell on deaf ears or were met with ridicule.

47

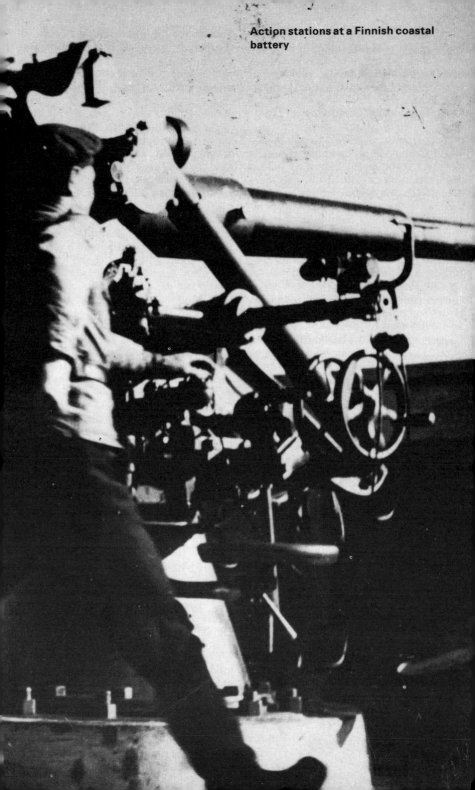

Action stations at a Finnish coastal battery

Even the majority of the Finnish Communists did not fall for his transparent blandishments and remained firmly committed to the defense of their fatherland against the Russians. The Finns were united in their belief that they were Finns first and rightists or leftists second, and no amount of propaganda or ideological appeals could change that. Intense nationalism, patriotism, and hatred of Russia precluded any possibility of collaboration with the fifth columnists.

At sea, the Russians proved themselves less than competent. Undefended islands along the coast were easily occupied, but every effort to land troops on the mainland was repulsed. The Russian Baltic Fleet shelled Porvoo, about eighteen miles east of Helsinki, in an effort to 'soften it up' for an amphibious landing, but was driven off by the shore batteries. Hanko and Turku also attracted the attention of the Soviet fleet, but to no avail. If Kruschev's memoirs are true, the Russian navy was so inept that it could not even distinguish a Swedish merchantman from a Finnish ship. According to Kruschev, a Soviet submarine fired upon an unarmed Swedish ship, mistaking it for a Finnish vessel, and failed to sink it. During the course of the war, three Russian destroyers, two submarines, and some auxiliary ships were either damaged or sunk by coastal batteries. In addition, the Russian battleship, *October Revolution*, was severely damaged.

The Russians did not fare much better in the air. During the first days of the war, their air raids failed to disrupt Finnish mobilization, which must have occasioned some surprise in the Soviet military establishment. Another problem was that the air attacks upon the major cities and communication lines were made with insufficient force and were hampered by the weather. Southern Finland in December enjoys about four hours of light each day, and the skies are frequently cloudy. A snowfall on the 2nd turned into a blizzard for two days thereafter, concealing all military targets while cloudy skies continued to hamper air operations until the middle of the month. But even when the weather cleared in January and February, the Soviet Air Force failed in its primary mission. Not even the one vital link Finland had with the outside world, the Kemi-Tornio railroad to Sweden, which carried Finland's exports as well as her imports of materials and weapons, was disrupted for more than a few hours at a time. Shipping traffic, especially from Turku, was rarely disrupted, despite sixty air raids upon the port facilities.

Moreover, despite their lack of new planes and adequate AA batteries, the Finns dealt the Soviet Air Force hard blows. At the outbreak of hostilities the Finns had ninety-six aircraft. During the war, the number rose to 287, 162 of which were fighters, while the Russians had about 2,500 by the end of the war with Finland. The Finns lost sixty-one planes as compared to Russian losses of 725 confirmed cases and 200 unconfirmed, according to Finnish military figures. Of these 314 were destroyed by AA batteries, and over 300 more were damaged. An indication of Finnish accuracy is that the average number of shots per downed plane was fifty-four for manual guns and 200 shots in the case of automatic weapons.

Considering the advantage the Russians enjoyed, the above facts and figures reveal the poor preparation and training which characterized the Russian Air Force. The matter is thrown into even sharper relief when one takes into account the distribution of Soviet air bases and their ready access to any place in Finland. Bomber bases were located in Estonia,

Above: A Finnish plane is prepared for take off. Finland lost sixty-one aircraft during the entire war. *Below:* Finnish AA gun crew inspect one of the 725 Russian airplanes which they shot down

The Fokker D XXI. Originally a Dutch design, the Fokker D XXI was operated by the Finnish Air Force, for which it was built under licence. The type, like many other machines operating in the Winter War, was obsolescent by Western standards, but proved capable of holdings its own against Russian fighters. Shortages of the Bristol Mercury engines by which the type was to be powered meant that the Finnish State Aircraft Factory had to redesign the nose to accommodate American Twin Wasp engines. *Engine :* one Pratt & Whitney Twin Wasp radial, 825-hp. *Armament :* four 7.9mm machine guns, with 300 rounds per gun. *Speed :* 272 mph at 9,000 feet. *Climb :* 4½ minutes to 9,840 feet. *Ceiling :* 32,000 feet. *Range :* 590 miles. *Weight empty/loaded :* 3,380/4,820 lbs. *Span :* 26 feet 1 inch. *Length :* 36 feet 3 inches.

The Fokker C V-E. The C V was used by the Finnish Air Force from 1927 until well into the Second World War as a reconnaissance machine and light bomber. It was totally outclassed by Soviet fighters, but survived by being used in remote areas and at low levels. The following performance and weight figures are for the 450-hp Lorraine-Dietrich powered C V-E. The Finnish example had a higher performance owing to their more powerful engines. *Engine :* one Bristol Pegasus IIM-2 radial, 730-hp. *Armament :* two 7.9mm machine guns and racks for several light bombs. *Speed :* 145 mph. *Climb :* 15.7 minutes to 13,120 feet. *Ceiling :* 21,500 feet. *Weight empty/loaded :* 3,058/4,158 lbs. *Span :* 45 feet 11¾ inches. *Length :* 27 feet 4¼ inches.

The Fokker C X. This Dutch reconnaissance and bomber aircraft first appeared in 1935, and served with the Dutch and Finnish Air Forces in the Second World War. The CX, like the CV which it was meant to supplant, was obsolete by world standards but survived by avoiding strong fighter opposition. *Engine :* one Bristol Pegasus XXI radial, 835-hp. *Armament :* two 7.9mm machine guns and up to 880 lbs of bombs. *Speed :* 212 mph at 10,000 feet. *Climb :* 9 minutes to 16,400 feet. *Ceiling :* 27,400 feet. *Range :* 520 miles. *Weight empty/loaded :* 3,410/5,500 lbs. *Span :* 39 feet 4 inches. *Length :* 30 feet 2 inches.

The Bristol Blenheim I. When introduced in 1935, the Blenheim light bomber was faster than most fighters in service at the time. Several examples were ordered by the Finns, and the type was also built under licence in Finland. It served with considerable distinction in the Winter War, though it was obsolescent by Western standards. Its chief failings were light armament and inadequate protection for fuel and crew. *Engines :* two Bristol Mercury VIII radials, 840-hp. *Armament :* two .303-inch machine guns and up to 1,000 lbs of bombs. *Speed :* 285 mph at 15,000 feet. *Climb :* 11½ minutes to 15,000 feet. *Ceiling :* 27,820 feet. *Range :* 1,125 miles. *Weight empty/loaded :* 8,100/12,500 lbs. *Span :* 56 feet 4 inches. *Length :* 39 feet 9 inches. *Crew :* three.

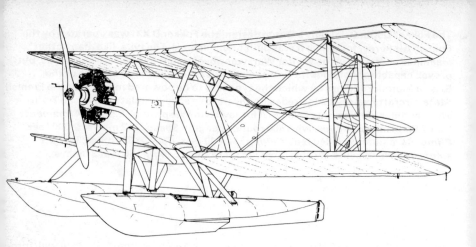

The Blackburn Ripon IIF. This version of Blackburn's standard torpedo and reconnaissance machine, which had first flown in 1926, was introduced in 1928. One example was built by the parent company for Finland, and a further twenty-five were built under licence in Finland between 1931 and 1934. The type was totally obsolete at the time of the Winter War. *Engine :* one Bristol Pegasus IIM 3 radial, 580-hp. *Armament :* two 7.9mm L-33 machine guns and one 18-inch torpedo or up to 1,650 lbs of bombs. *Speed :* 118mph at 5,000 feet. *Climb :* 360 feet per minute initially. *Ceiling :* 8,700 feet. *Range :* 1,284 miles as a reconnaissance aircraft. *Weight empty/loaded :* 4,311/7,461 lbs. *Span :* 45 feet 6½ inches. *Length :* 39 feet 4 inches.

The Bristol Bulldog IVA. This was the last mark of the famous interwar biplane fighter to be built in any numbers, to a Finnish order for seventeen. They served with considerable gallantry against superior opposition in 1939/1940. *Engine : one Bristol Mercury* VIS 2 radial, 775-hp. *Armament :* two 7.9mm machine guns. *Speed :* 224 mph. *Ceiling :* 33,400 feet. *Climb :* 13 minutes to 20,000 feet. *Weight empty/loaded :* 2,690/4,010 lbs. *Span :* 33 feet 8 inches. *Length :* 25 feet 4 inches.

near Leningrad, and in East Karelia, so that weather seldom made all air operations impossible. Arctic weather should not have handicapped the Russian pilots either, because of their experience under these conditions. Moreover, the unusually clear weather after mid-December made possible heavier air raids than would have been the case during a normal winter. In all, about 150,000 explosive and incendiary bombs were loosed on the country – a total of about 7,500 tons.

Civilians in Helsinki take refuge in the city's sewers during a Russian air-raid

Like the Londoners of the Second World War, however, the people of Finland were not to be cowed; they took the matter calmly and went about their business. An American journalist covering the war relates how, when the air raid sirens went off, the maid in his hotel would come in and sing out in English: 'Molotov is here!'

The terror of
the tanks

If the situation was in hand on the Isthmus, the same could not be said about the sixty-mile front north of Lake Ladoga. There, matters had become extremely critical. Two Finnish divisions, with very few anti-tank guns, were stretched over the front from Salmi to Suojärvi, facing the Red Eighth Army with its nine divisions and a tank brigade. The Soviet forces were divided into four columns whose objectives were Ilomantsi, Tolvajärvi, Suojärvi, and Sortavala. With these goals achieved they would have control of the Sortavala-Joensuu-Oulu railroad and the internal communications and transportation networks of Finland. Further north, the Red forces were rapidly advancing on Kuhmo and Suomussalmi, threatening to cut the nation in two.

Fearing a general and massive attack upon the Isthmus, the Finnish High Command had intended to hold its reserves for that contingency in the hope that the northern front would hold. Confronted by the crisis in the north, however, and the peril to the rail network, reinforcements from the meager reserves near Viipuri and Oulu were rushed to Tolvajärvi, Kuhmo, and Suomussalmi. On 5th December, Mannerheim ordered the 16th Infantry Regiment and a detachment to Kuhmo and Suomussalmi, where a battalion had already pre-

A Finnish artilleryman at Kollaa directs fire upon the advancing Russian tanks

57

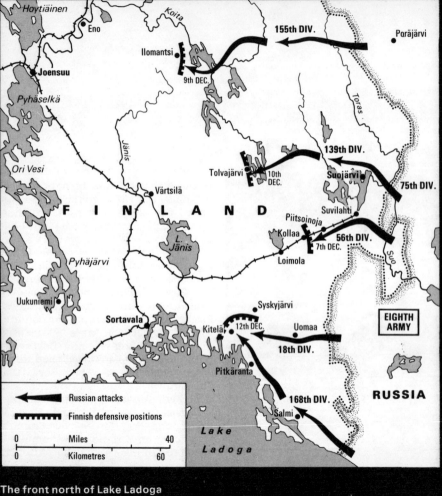

The front north of Lake Ladoga

ceded them. Three depot battalions, Detachment 'A', a quickly organized and poorly equipped ski group, were sent to the Ilomantsi sector north of Salmi, and another battalion to Salla, in the far north.

According to operational plans based on peacetime maneuvers, Finnish forces immediately north of Ladoga were to withdraw from Salmi to Kitelä and then launch a counterattack on the enemy's flanks from the direction of Loimola-Syskyjärvi as he advanced along the lakeshore. Hence, the Soviet advance up to Kitelä occasioned no dismay. However, the Finnish operational plan was jeopardized by the prospect of an enemy advance along the Suojärvi railroad and the roads from Suojärvi to Ilomantsi and Tolvajärvi.

The most immediate threat was in the Suojärvi sector, due to the rapid advance of the Red armored columns. By 2nd December the Finns had retreated from Suvilahti to prepared positions at Piitsoinoja. Orders were issued on the 3rd for a counterattack to regain Suvilahti, but the operation evaporated in the face of the Russian tanks. Erkki Palolampi, an eyewitness, records in his book, *Kollaa kestää*, how the Finnish anti-tank

units had at first held the Russians back and accounted for twenty-three tanks on the road. However, it was impossible to stop the Red assault and 'The rumble of tanks was heard on the road and also moving in the woods . . . Someone began shouting that the tanks were shooting from the rear! They have broken through! One man was wide-eyed with terror, others saw his panic, shouts passed from man to man so that nothing could prevent it: Tanks are coming, the tanks have broken through! The men began to run, wading in the snow and skiing toward the rear without concern for anything, heedless of their officers' shouts and curses. The panic spread, other companies bolted . . . rumors flew . . . everyone had but one aim – to get away from the terror of the tanks . . . A young soldier attempting to jump on a sled shouted out: "Now, not even the Finns can handle the Russians!" '

By the 7th, the prepared positions at Piitsoinoja had been completely abandoned and the troops had withdrawn to the secondary line at Kollaa.

Tank-traps at Kollaa, behind which the Finns retired to regroup and counterattack

The Russian T35 heavy assault tank. The requirement for this weapon was originated
in 1932, the idea behind the specification clearly being to produce a Russian tank
similar to the French Char 2C. The tank was intended to operate against infantry
and anti-tanks guns, being fitted with a howitzer in the main turret for use against
the former, and 45mm guns in the off-side front and near-side rear of the four
subsidiary turrets grouped around the main one for use against the latter. By the
time of the Winter War, the T35's armor had been increased considerably,
and the early pattern 45mm guns had been replaced by ones of higher muzzle
velocity to enable them to deal with improved anti-tank weapons.

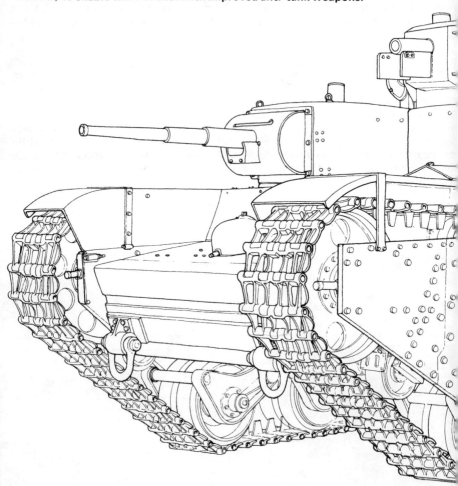

Crew : 10. *Armament :* One 76.2mm howitzer with 100 rounds, two 45mm guns with 26 rounds and five 7.62mm machine guns with 10,000 rounds. *Armor :* 50mm maximum and 11mm minimum. *Speed :* 18mph. *Radius of action :* 93 miles. *Power :* M17 12-cylinder engine, 500hp at 1450rpm. *Length :* 32 feet 4 inches. *Height :* 1 feet 4 inches. *Width :* 10 feet 8 inches. *Weight :* 50 tons.

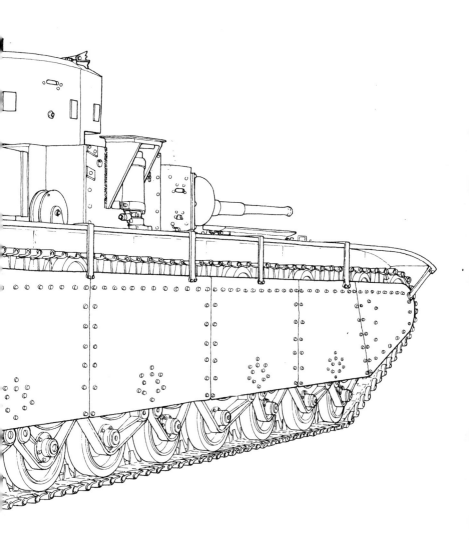

Left: Major-General J V Hägglund, commander of the Sortavala-Suojärvi sector. *Right:* Colonel (here Major-General) Paavo Talvela who was transferred to command the Ilomantsi-Tolvajärvi front

It was essential that Kollaa be held, lest the entire plan of counterattack should fail. The Russians started a massive attack on the 7th but were stopped, and the situation was so well stabilized by the 10th that the threat was over for the time being.

As the bad news poured in from the Ladoga front, Mannerheim decided the situation was too overwhelming and critical for one man to handle. On 5th December he divided the command, leaving Major-General Hägglund in command of the Sorta-vala-Suojärvi sector and posting Colonel Paavo Talvela, an officer of great courage and determination, to the Ilomantsi-Tolvajärvi area.

A man of Talvela's character was essential, for he was ordered to assume the offensive and defeat the enemy with numerically inferior forces, who could receive no reinforcements other than those already on their way. Moreover, except for the reserve battalion sent in by Hägglund shortly

before, his troops already fighting in the area – three battalions at Tolva-järvi and one at Ilomantsi – were exhausted by their struggle against two Red divisions.

Already during the first days of combat, the one battalion defending Tolvajärvi against the Red 139th Division had been forced to withdraw to the Aitto River, where it was joined by a second battalion. An attempted counterattack by the combined battalions failed. Unable to withstand the Russian firepower, the forces found it necessary to retreat to the west side of Lake Aglä the next day. Here a third battalion joined the fight. Aided by the frozen ground, the Soviet offensive moved forward, forcing another retreat on the 5th, which took the Finns to a position just east of Tolvajärvi. In the view of the Finnish commanding officers, the men were beginning to lose their fitness for battle, and a catastrophe was approaching.

When Talvela arrived on the scene, he decided that a radical change in operations was necessary to avert disaster. He accordingly ordered Lieutenant-Colonel A O Pajari to lead a reinforced battalion deep behind the enemy lines to make an attack on the night of 8th December. Pajari carried out his orders to the letter, inflicting heavy losses on the enemy and paralyzing the Russians for a couple of days. Then, on the 11th, unobserved by Finnish scouts, the Russians attempted an outflanking operation around the northern end of the lake and attacked a supply column. Pajari, who happened to be passing by, quickly gathered a group of men from the supply detachments and attacked the enemy, aided by a couple of companies from the front line reserves. By nightfall, the Russians were routed and pursued into the woods where those who were not killed by Finnish soldiers died from the cold. These successes improved the morale of the Finns, and the next day a Red frontal attack was repulsed.

At the same time, the situation near Ilomansi was brought under control. After the initial withdrawals had been accomplished, the poorly equipped Detachment 'A' arrived. The presence of these reinforcements proved decisive. Because the Finnish position was well placed and strong, it withstood the Soviet attack on the 9th. The following day the Finns launched an attack of their own and succeeded in surrounding the Soviet battalion, which was completely annihilated.

Having stopped the Soviet advance on Tolvajärvi, Talvela assumed the initiative on the 12th. In these operations the severe cold, as low as — 40 degrees Fahrenheit, the dense forests, and surprise were to prove decisive for the Finns. According to Talvela's battle plan, a double pincer movement with the stronger wing to the north, was to encircle the Russians and hold them until the lack of supplies and the extreme temperatures did their work.

Almost immediately, it became clear that the original Finnish plan would not succeed, since the Russians were engaged in a pincer movement of their own on the east side of Lakes Tolva and Hirvas, which made contact with the Finnish left wing. The Finnish right wing also ran into difficulties as

Lieutenant-Colonel A O Pajari

it tried to cross Lake Tolva. Unable to complete the crossing the Finns, nevertheless, managed to seize Koti Island, thus bringing the enemy's rear and communications under fire.

Both sides were momentarily checked by their inability to complete their encirclements, until Pajari decided upon a bold frontal attack across the ice on the northern end of Lake Tolva. Pajari's move gave the Finns a victory of the first magnitude, for it made possible the total destruction of the Russian forces in that area. The vanguard of the attack was a company led by a wounded lieutenant; when the fighting was over only eight men remained alive. By the 14th the entire Tolvajärvi sector was in Finnish hands and the Red 139th Division was completely routed. There was no doubt about the decisiveness of the victory: the Russians had lost 1,000 dead, several hundred prisoners, ten tanks, two batteries, and large quantities of supplies and small arms. Although they were too exhausted to pursue their defeated foe, the Finnish troops had to continue the fight for another ten days.

A fresh Russian division, the 75th,

was sent in to extricate the battered 139th and seize the road to Agläjärvi, which was the only supply route the Russians had. Realizing their danger, the Finnish troops advanced from Tolvajärvi towards the oncoming Russians. Unaccustomed to forest fighting, the Russians found themselves overwhelmed by Finnish guerrilla tactics and by frontal attacks. By the 18th, the village of Agläjärvi, which had been strongly fortified by the Russians, was in Finnish hands, and the enemy was in full retreat. The Finns pressed their advantage and pursued the remnants of the 139th and 75th Divisions to the Aitto River, where they were destroyed almost to a man.

Tolvajärvi was a remarkable victory for the Finns and is even more startling when one considers the other statistics of Russian losses. For the Finns it meant a windfall of sixty tanks, over thirty field guns, ten grenade launchers, almost 400 machine guns, and large quantities of munitions and supplies. In addition, countless weapons and large quantities of equipment were destroyed during the battle. Finnish losses, however, were proportionately high – so high, in fact, that Mannerheim had at one point seriously considered ordering a halt to the battle. But, at the insistence of the commanders on the front, he had allowed the battle to continue to its conclusion. In the end, thirty per cent of the officers and non-commissioned officers and thirty-five per cent of the enlisted personnel were killed or wounded.

Meanwhile, the Ilomantsi sector had also stabilized. Four weak battalions and a single battery had met the Russian 15th Division and stopped it cold. This sector was to remain stable for

Dead Russians from the rout of the Red 139th Division

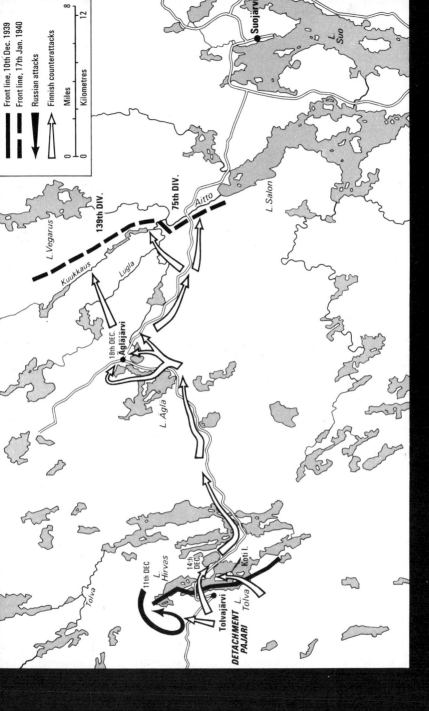

The Tolvajärvi-Suojärvi front

Front line, 10th Dec. 1939
Front line, 17th Jan. 1940
Russian attacks
Finnish counterattacks

Miles
Kilometres

0   8   12

Suojärvi

L. Suo

139th DIV.

75th DIV.

L. Vegarus

Kuukkaus

Lugla

Aitto

L. Salon

18th DEC.
Äglajärvi

L. Agla

11th DEC

L. Hirvas

Tolva

14th DEC.

L. Koti I.

Tolvajärvi

L. Tolva

DETACHMENT
PAJARI

The limited maneuverability of Soviet armor in the forested areas of Finland enabled the defenders to break down the Russian columns into manageable *mottis*

the duration of the war.

These successes were a great morale booster for the hard-pressed Finns, especially on the north-east shore of Lake Ladoga, where the Russian 168th and 18th Divisions had penetrated the Finnish lines on 8th December. By the 12th, a Finnish counterattack had straightened out the line again and forced the Russians to withdraw. With Kollaa holding, hopes were high that the two Russian divisions could be surrounded and destroyed.

Finnish attacking groups were positioned in a U-shape from Kitelä to Uomaa, and the prospects for annihilating the enemy divisions looked good. However, the first two attacks on 13th and 17th December failed as the intense cold, the weariness of the troops, the lack of sufficient equipment, and superior Russian firepower began to take their toll of IV Army Corps. Finally, on 26th December, one Finnish group successfully attacked the Russian positions east of Lake Kota. On the 27th, the Uomaa highway came under Finnish fire and the cord-

on was gradually drawn tighter around the enemy. After regrouping his forces and being assured tha Kollaa was still holding, Hägglund prepared for the final operations against the 168th and 18th Divisions. The plan called for breaking up the Russian forces into small isolated groups called *mottis*, (a term usually used to mean wood piled up for chopping), by means of guerrilla tactics. During the night of 5th January, IV Army Corps was moved through a virtually roadless, snow-covered, wooded area – the terrain seriously hampering the movement of heavy equipment – to its staging areas. On the 6th the attack began. Apparently unaware of what was happening, the Russians attempted neither a counterattack nor a withdrawal from the areas as the Finns closed in. Instead, they dug in and prepared to hold out where they were. By the 11th, the Russians were completely surrounded and divided into *mottis*, between which the Finns moved with impunity.

Everything had gone according to plan, and the Finns were justified in believing that it would be only a matter of time before the Russians laid down their arms. But they had underestimated the toughness of their adversary who stubbornly held out behind the

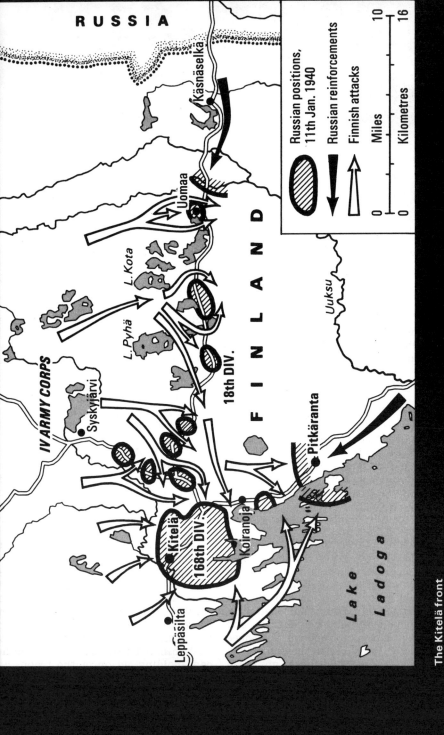

The Kitelä front

Russian tanks in action in the Kollaa area

tanks, which they had dug in at the perimeter of the defenses, placing the artillery in the center. Hunger also plagued them since only inadequate supplies could be airlifted in, and as a result, they were reduced to eating their horses. If the Finns had had more field artillery and anti-tank guns, the problem would have been resolved sooner. As it was, IV Army ·Corps spent the rest of January and part of February trying to destroy the *mottis*, while at the same time fending off four new Red divisions advancing from Salmi and Käsnäselkä.

The only solution for the Finns was to deal with one *motti* at a time, making sure all communications with it were sealed off, and then annihilating it. In this manner, the 18th Division's ten *mottis* were gradually wiped out. On 18th February, what was left of the 18th Division surrendered and its tank brigade followed suit on the 29th. On the battlefield 4,300 Russian dead were counted, including two generals, but this figure does not account for those who were lying under the snow. The booty included 128 tanks, 91 guns, 120 cars and tractors, 62 field kitchens, and huge quantities of infantry weapons, munitions, and equipment.

Only the end of the war spared the 168th Division the same fate. Supplied from the air and even by horse-drawn vehicles from across Lake Ladoga, which were protected by tanks, the division desperately held out. The fate of the supply columns across the lake, however, showed the folly of this: a few Finnish soldiers on an island just off Koiranoja undertook a series of night battles against the columns and succeeded in destroying most of them before an attack from the mainland and from the air completely wiped them out.

In the Kollaa sector the few weak battalions carried on their uneven struggle with complete success and halted the enemy's advance, thus relieving the pressure on IV Army Corps. Although almost reeling from exhaustion, the defenders held their positions without relief throughout January, except for some small reinforcements consisting of three independent battalions, a regiment, and a cavalry brigade, which had been converted into a ski brigade. None of these troops were able to leave the front lines during this period for a well-deserved rest. But the magnificent holding action of the troops at Kollaa made possible the triumph of Hägglund's forces further south.

That the Russians were stopped on

the Isthmus and north of Lake Ladoga was probably due as much to the determination of the defenders as it was to the ineffectiveness of the Red Army. There is no doubt that the Russian soldier was brave, but the tactics employed by his superiors cancelled out much of his effectiveness. However, the Russian soldier was not as resourceful as his Finnish counterpart and was unable to function effectively in the extraordinary situation he found in the war against Finland. It

Ammunition is brought up for the defense of the Kollaa river

was also evident that the Russians did not plan their attacks properly to obtain the maximum cooperation and coordination of the various detachments attached to the divisions. Artillery fire was so poorly aimed that much of it went far over the heads of the Finns. There were times when the tanks advanced to the Finnish positions and then returned before the infantry had even begun its advance. This sort of ineffectiveness and lack of coordination continued throughout December, until Marshal Timoshenko assumed command of the Red Army in Finland.

Another factor which made the Russian losses so astounding was the inability of the Red commanders to change their tactics according to the needs of time and space. Instead, they adhered blindly to the original plan, sending wave after wave of human beings to the slaughter without hesitation, seemingly unable to devise any other mode of attack than that of brute force.

Marshal S Timoshenko's appointment as commander of the Red Armies in Finland finally brings coordination to the Soviet offensive

Determined
defenders

Despite the difficulties and hardships which the magnitude of the invading forces caused in the delaying operations on the Karelian Isthmus, the covering troops had bought time for their compatriots to move into primary defensive positions. After the covering troops were withdrawn from the forward positions on 6th December, there were a few days of relative quiet along the front, as the Red forces regrouped.

Only sporadic probing missions and artillery fire disturbed the calm but this action was sufficient to alarm the untried troops of the newly arrived field army. Operating mostly in the darkness without adequate lighting – they did not even have enough flashlights – it is not surprising that the untried troops were nervous. Fortunately, the period of quiet gave them a chance to get accustomed to front line life. Even the troops behind the lines were apprehensive, and for good reason – the front line was so shallow that it is almost incredible that Russian patrols never found their way to the rear.

If the Russians launched only a small number of mass attacks, their patrols were busy probing, and these operations provoked many a night's skirmish with the defenders. More-

The Mannerheim Line on the Karelian Isthmus

Finnish firing-line at Summa

over, they occasionally succeeded in cutting through the barbed wire in order to blow up or drag away the boulders serving as tank traps. These Russian activities quickly brought home to the Finns the fact that the tank traps were placed too far forward from the bunkers, therefore making it difficult to guard them effectively, especially in the dark. It was now too late to rectify the error.

Although the period of Soviet passivity was invaluable to the Finns, giving them a chance to get their 'second wind', as well as to reorganize and regroup their forces, at the same time the Russians were bringing up additional forces and regrouping them, familiarizing them with the operations and planning their attack. From the activity among the Red forces it became clear that they contemplated a two-pronged attack; one directed at Summa, the Viipuri Gateway, and the other toward Taipale on the extreme eastern end of the Mannerheim Line. Obviously, the Summa attack was of crucial importance for both sides, since, if the attack succeeded, it would open the road to Viipuri and Helsinki and the Finnish heartland, thus bringing an end to the war by crushing the majority of Finnish forces in a gigantic pincer movement. The attack on Taipale was

apparently a feint to draw the Finns away from the primary objective. Moreover, with the good road network in the area and the use of Lake Ladoga, the Russians were able to move on Taipale first. Consequently, during the night of 14th December, Finnish patrols reported that the Russians were preparing to attack. The one enemy infantry division already there had been joined by a second, along with more artillery.

Early in the morning of 15th December, the Russians began pounding the Finnish positions with artillery. It was up to the Finnish infantry to hold the line in spite of the severity of the barrage, however, since the Finnish batteries had few guns and shells, and the guns they possessed had a very short range. Hence, the Finnish plan called for holding fire until the enemy emerged into the open on the ice and then firing at them at almost point-blank range. When the battle ended, the Russians had been driven back with a loss of twelve tanks and inummerable dead.

After a day of comparative inactivity, the Russians attacked again on the 17th, and the same day a massive effort was made to breach the position at Summa. Wave after wave of Russian soldiers was hurled against the Fin-

Russian strong-points provide bases for further assaults on the Isthmus

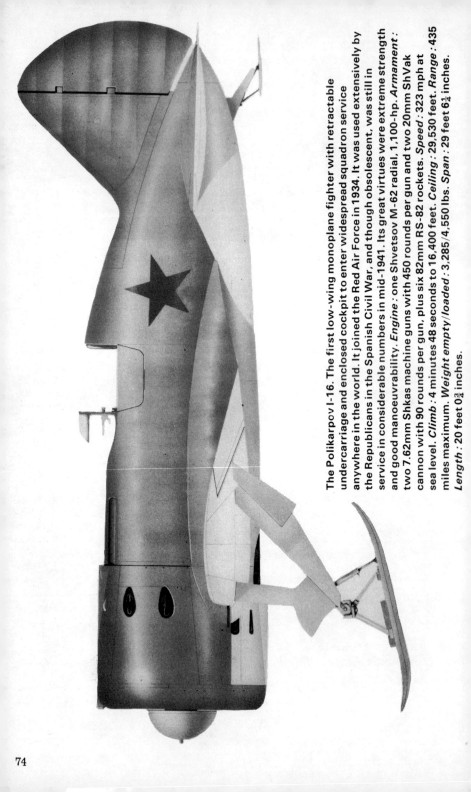

The Polikarpov I-16. The first low-wing monoplane fighter with retractable undercarriage and enclosed cockpit to enter widespread squadron service anywhere in the world. It joined the Red Air Force in 1934. It was used extensively by the Republicans in the Spanish Civil War, and though obsolescent, was still in service in considerable numbers in mid-1941. Its great virtues were extreme strength and good manoeuvrability. *Engine*: one Shvetsov M-62 radial, 1,100-hp. *Armament*: two 7.62mm Shkas machine guns with 450 rounds per gun and two 20mm ShVak cannon with 90 rounds per gun, plus six 82mm RS-82 rockets. *Speed*: 323 mph at sea level. *Climb*: 4 minutes 48 seconds to 16,400 feet. *Ceiling*: 29,530 feet. *Range*: 435 miles maximum. *Weight empty/loaded*: 3,285/4,550 lbs. *Span*: 29 feet 6¼ inches. *Length*: 20 feet 0¾ inches.

nish lines while the Finns held their fire until the enemy was within some fifty yards. Still the Russian commanders ordered their troops forward in an almost criminal disregard for human life. Finally, the Soviet troops could take no more and fled in blind panic. Thereafter, the Red attacks at Taipale, beginning on Christmas Day and continuing through the 27th, were haphazard and uncoordinated. A small change in Russian operational plans did reveal itself during these attacks: they moved the attack from the south to the west side of the Finnish defenses but little was accomplished by this maneuver except an increase in the enemy dead. Furthermore, little damage was done to the Finnish lines, or to their guns.

While the attack on Taipale was under way, a major offensive was being prepared in the Summa area. The Russians launched numerous probing missions, during which they rapidly built up their forces behind the lines. By mid-December, it was evident that a full-scale attack, designed to end the war quickly, was imminent.

To the Finnish command, the situation appeared extremely critical. The entire 5th Division was deployed on a long, thin line with very few reserves to back it up. The reserve of the Commander-in-Chief, the 6th Division, was so distant from the front as to negate its value to the threatened sector. With insufficient artillery and the shortage of shells, any sort of counteroffensive was considered too dangerous and costly. Little could be done, therefore, other than to regroup the forces and await the onslaught.

The beginning of the offensive was announced by a heavy artillery barrage in the early hours of 17th December. At 10 am came the attack itself. A full division was thrown into the assault and was supported by airplanes and about eighty tanks. Advancing behind the tanks, the Russian infantry marched bravely into the hail of Finnish fire, seemingly oblivious to the havoc around them. For the defenders,

it was a horrifying experience which tested their nerves to the fullest as the enemy fell in heaps in front of their eyes. A further strain was the presence of tanks, which, because of the modest artillery available and the lack of anti-tank guns, could not be stopped completely. (In the daylight it was difficult, if not impossible, to deliver 'Molotov cocktails'). Another handicap was the disruption of the telephone communications by enemy fire; as a result, the command post could not communicate with the various sectors except by using old radio equipment, which did not always function.

It was only after nightfall, when the Russian guns fell silent and the telephone wires were repaired, that a full assessment of the day's activities could be made. When the field commanders were able to communicate with one another again, they spoke in a jargon which had been developed in the few weeks of war in order to confuse the enemy but which avoided the use of code, which took too long to decipher. The jargon was a fusion of Finnish and Swedish, combined with pet names for their own groups and acquaintances. From the reports that came in it was clear that at the only point where the enemy had penetrated the lines, into Summa village, he had been thrown back in the first hours of darkness. When the Russians withdrew, they had twenty-five tanks less than when they started and an unconscionable number of casualties.

Undaunted by their losses, the Russians renewed the attack the next day after a five-hour barrage. Some seventy tanks were used in the assault, but the Finnish fire proved so accurate in the opening phase that ten tanks were knocked out almost immediately, stopping the attack before it got started. Unable to break the Finnish resistance by frontal attack, the Russians continued to fire upon the lines throughout the night.

The following day, 19th December, saw the beginning of the heaviest attack of the war to that time. Six divisions, an armored army corps, and two tank brigades were hurled against the Finnish positions, while bombers and fighters gave them air support. This time the attack was on a broader front but with the main thrust concentrated on Summa. At that point, the attack was so massive and the tank commanders so oblivious to their own danger that the tanks broke through the obstacles and beyond the Finnish lines. Later, reports from Summa said that there were about 100 tanks operating there at once, but no one knew it at the time since the communication lines had again been cut. One thing the Finns learned from this battle, albeit too late to do anything, was that the boulders used as tank traps were not large enough. But in spite of the breakthrough and the severity of the attack, the breach was sealed and the enemy repulsed.

In other sections, the Russians fared no better. On the road north of Summa, the Red tanks found themselves in such a thick forest on either side of the road that they could not leave it and

Finnish defenders await the assault of six Russian divisions on the Summa front

were forced to proceed almost literally into the mouths of Finnish cannons. It was not until the next night that the survivors were able to turn round and withdraw.

Throughout that day and the next, the Russians continued their attacks with a constant supply of fresh troops to replace the fallen. By this time, the Russian artillery was improving its aim, thus aiding the advancing tanks and infantry more effectively than earlier. (In the first phases of the war the enemy artillery had been so poorly aimed that most of the shots went far over the heads of the Finns.) Despite these improvements, however, the Finns were still in their positions when the attacks ended on the 23rd. Surveying the battlefield afterwards, they could not doubt that the Russians had suffered a severe defeat, for innumerable dead lay among the fifty-eight tanks lying smashed behind and in front of the lines. Thus far, the Finns had destroyed 239 tanks on the Isthmus alone.

Any number of reasons could be given for the poor showing of the Red forces, but four seem most salient. Firstly, the Russians had assumed there would be little or no resistance and therefore had not planned their

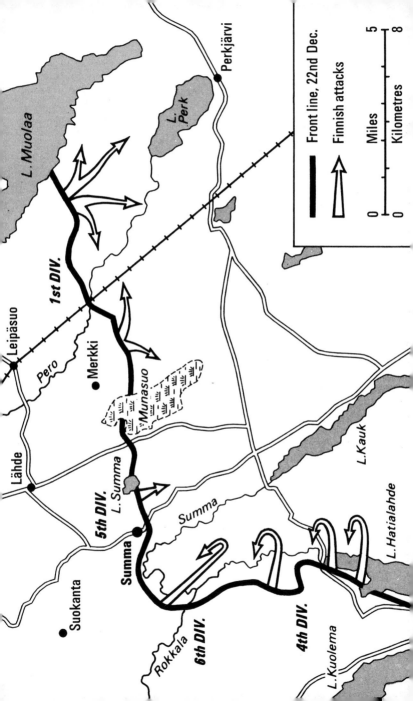

The Finns counterattack south of Lake Muolaa

operations carefully enough. Apparently, they believed brute force would be sufficient. Secondly, they remained blindly committed to their original plan and failed to alter it under the changed conditions of actual war, apparently believing that more tanks and more men would compensate for lack of foresight. Thirdly, the Russian commanders were subordinate to the authority of the political officers attached to the units and therefore feared to make decisions which might lead to their being politically suspect: the specter of the purges still haunted the Red Army. Finally, besides being competently led, the Finns were fighting for their own homes; as a result, they stood up better under the stress of battle than the Soviet soldiers who not only were poorly trained and led but also had been led to believe that they would be welcomed with open arms by the Finns, rather than having to fight them. Moreover, the Russian soldiers were facing combat in a strange and, for them, hostile environment. Many of them had never been in a forest of any size, having lived only on the plains of Russia. Then, too, the Finns were dressed in white, while their Russian counterparts were clothed in field grey, which made them stand out like chimney sweeps in the snow.

Having stopped the Russian advance dead, it was now the turn of the Finns to attack. Already, during the delaying operations, Major-General Öhquist had requested permission for such an operation with II Army Corps, but his proposal had been turned down as too risky at the time. When his proposal was resubmitted during the battle at Summa, it was approved by the Finnish High Command on the 19th.

According to the plan, the 6th Division, which was lying in reserve behind Summa, reinforced by an infantry regiment, was to join parts of five other divisions in the offensive. The attack was to take place between Lakes Muola and Kuolema on about a fifteen-mile front. On the west end of the line, parts of the 4th Division were to advance on the right wing of the 6th Division, which was to move along the Summa River. Parts of the 5th Division would be responsible for tying down the Russians in the vicinity of Summa. At the eastern end of the line, groups from the 1st Division were to attack along the railroad, while further east, parts of the 11th Division were to penetrate westward to catch the Russians between them and the 1st Division

units.

This was an ambitious plan, indeed. If it succeeded the Finns might be in a position to bargain with the Kremlin for a peaceful settlement of the conflict – not that the Finnish commanders expected to have a total triumph: they would content themselves with somewhat less than complete victory if their offensive disturbed the enemy sufficiently, causing him to lose some ground and to reconsider the whole situation.

Zero hour was set for 6.30 am on 23rd December. When the time arrived, snow was falling but it soon stopped, after which the temperature fell to – 4 degrees Fahrenheit, the wind rose, and the efficiency of the troops diminished. Under these circumstances, it quickly became obvious that the counterattack would not proceed as well as planned. Other problems soon became apparent. In some instances, the reserve forces brought up for the operation had too many vehicles with them and were still trying to get them transferred only hours before the beginning of the attack. Adequate reconnaissance of the enemy's positions had not been undertaken prior to the attack, and the exact locations of his positions and dispositions of men and weapons were unknown.

At first the Finnish attackers met

Russian snipers in action

with little resistance, but then the Russian tanks moved in, putting a stop to the advance. Once again, communications were disrupted by cut wires and improperly functioning radios, so close cooperation between various attack groups broke down. In addition, since the artillery could not move up as fast as the infantry, there was little opportunity to use the big guns against the tanks in support of the infantry; when the guns did arrive it was unknown where they were needed most because of lack of communications. After eight hours, the offensive was called off, and the Finns withdrew to their own lines without interference.

Although the counterattack was hardly a success, it did improve the morale of the troops and, perhaps more importantly, it shook up the enemy. Given the numerical inferiority of the Finns, compounded by their inadequate firepower and communications system, it is surprising that they even attempted the operation. However, the Russians made no effort to renew their attacks on the Isthmus for over a month, except for sporadic sorties at Taipale from 25th to 27th December and minor skirmishes along the line in January.

The battle of Suomussalmi

Midway between the Arctic Sea and the Karelian Isthmus is a sparsely populated area on the eastern frontier of Finland where some of the most celebrated battles of the Winter War were fought. Here, in the vicinity of the tiny villages of Suomussalmi and Kuhmo, three Red divisions met their doom at the hands of the small Finnish force.

Believing that the Russians would make no major efforts in this virtually roadless wilderness, the Finnish High Command had left the defenses there to a handful of men from the reserves, border guards, and Civic Guard units. When it was realized that the enemy was not only invading the areas but was doing so with two divisions and the usual complement of tanks and that he had an additional division waiting in the wings, reinforcements were rushed to the front. Here, as behind the border at Ladoga, the Russians had been busy building new roads leading to the frontier; over these they now poured into Finland.

The people in the area were firmly convinced that because of their isolation, they had nothing to fear from Russia; hence, although they had known for some time that the Russians were concentrating troops on the other side of the border, they con-

The Finns deploy prior to the destruction of two Soviet divisions around Suomussalmi

Units of the 25th Regiment from Oulu's 9th Division move up to reinforce the defenders of Kuhmo

tinued working and sending their children to school right up to the day of the invasion. The populace only began to evacuate the region on 30th November, when the Russians were already upon them. This situation occasioned a great deal of suffering and economic loss to the civilian populace; in some instances, children had to flee from school when the Russians were at the door.

In the vicinity of Kuhmo, parts of the Russian 54th Division were advancing along the two roads leading to that village. Only a battalion of defenders stood in their path, but despite their limited numbers and resources, the Finns began flank attacks on 1st December. Unable to halt the enemy's march, they were forced to retreat to positions further back, only to find themselves compelled to withdraw again on the 5th. At this stage, it became apparent that the situation was critical and the forces badly in need of reinforcements, so the 25th Regiment from Oulu's 9th Division was dispatched to the sector. These fresh troops were equipped only with rifles, machine guns, tents, and their omnipresent skis; they had no field guns or anti-tank weapons since none were available. Immediately upon their arrival, the reinforcements were thrown into combat, before the Russians had time to receive additional troops or to strengthen their positions.

Time was of the essence, and the Finns renewed their attacks on the Russian flanks before they had even completed all their preparations or the new arrivals had had time to become familiar with the situation. On 8th December, an assault from north and south of the Kuhmo road succeeded in cutting the enemy column into several

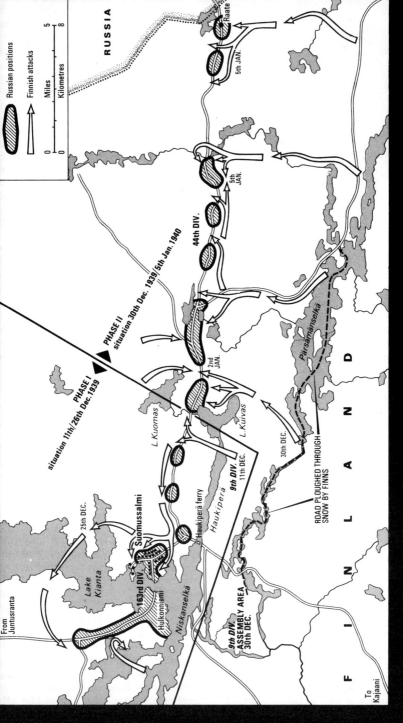

The destruction of the Russian 163rd and 44th Divisions at Suomussalmi

Map labels:

Russian positions

Finnish attacks

Miles / Kilometres
0 — 5
0 — 8

RUSSIA

Raate
5th JAN.
5th JAN.

44th DIV.
5th JAN.

PHASE II
situation 30th Dec. 1939/5th Jan. 1940

PHASE I
situation 11th/26th Dec. 1939

2nd JAN.

L. Kuomas

L. Kuivas

Parsamanselkä

FINLAND

ROAD PLOUGHED THROUGH
SNOW BY FINNS

30th DEC.

9th DIV.
11th DEC.

Haukiperä ferry
Haukiperä

9th DIV.
ASSEMBLY AREA
30th DEC.

Niskanselkä

Hulkonniemi

163rd DIV

Suomussalmi

Lake
Kianta

25th DEC.

From
Juntusranta

To
Kajaani

Colonel H J Siilasvuo, the victor of Suomussalmi

sections. For a time, the Finns were able to maintain control over these groups, but gradually fatigue, casualties, difficulties of support, and the lack of field telephones, which made it almost impossible to coordinate the operations, compelled the Finns to abandon their efforts and leave the Russians in possession of the road. Another handicap was the weather, which had turned extremely cold, with temperatures falling as low as — 22 degrees Fahrenheit. But at least these operations stopped the Russian advance and, by the 20th, the front was stabilized. For the Russians it was a difficult time and probably an embarrassing predicament: they could not move forward, and they dared not withdraw. At the same time, they were unable to come to grips with the Finns, who moved ghost-like on their skis through the snow-laden forests and seemed to strike at will, when and where they pleased. Apparently these tactics accounted in part for the passivity of the Russians and their failure to mount any heavy attacks against

the Finnish positions. Instead, they dug in along the road where, exposed to the freezing weather, they began the long wait for the rest of the 54th Division to come and extricate them from their plight. By the end of January, they faced an even greater menace when additional Finnish troops, fresh from their victory at Suomussalmi, arrived.

Some fifty miles north of Kuhmo, near the village of Suomussalmi, there took place one of the classic battles in military history. A Finnish force of approximately a division engaged two complete Red divisions (the 163rd and 44th) and annihilated them almost to a man.

Across the border from Soumussalmi, as elsewhere, and without the knowledge of the Finns, the Russians had constructed new roads leading to the border. These roads enabled them to advance with remarkably strong forces into otherwise roadless territory. There were two main roads converging on Suomussalmi from the east: one began near Juntusranta in the north, and the other at Raate, further south. From the Suomussalmi junction the road continued on to Kajaani, through which passed the highway and railroad leading to Oulu, Tornio and Sweden. Two Russian regiments advanced on the northern road while a third moved along the Raate road; thus, the entire 163rd Ukranian Division was directed against one Finnish reserve battalion.

Since the odds were so great, the covering troops only engaged in light harassment of the enemy columns while they waited for reinforcements. Operating in two groups, the Finnish battalion slowly retreated along both roads until they came together again in Suomussalmi on 6th December. The next day, after putting the village to the torch, the battalion retreated to positions across a narrow lake which was not yet frozen hard enough to bear the weight of tanks. From there they watched the Russian columns come together in what was left of the village, knowing full well that they were the only obstacle between the Russians and an advance on Oulu.

By this time, Colonel Siilasvuo was on his way to the sector with the 27th Infantry Regiment from Oulu's 9th Division. Siilasvuo had been appointed commander of all the forces to operate in the Suomussalmi sector. The arrival of his troops was delayed, however, when the train carrying them struck a supply train, blocking the rail line for more than twenty-four hours. Nevertheless, since the newly completed section of the railroad came within twenty-five miles of Suomussalmi, Siilasvuo was still able to arrive on the 9th and commence counteroperations on the 11th.

After sizing up the situation and learning the disposition of the enemy, Siilasvuo ordered a weakly reinforced detachment to move north-west of Suomussalmi for an attack on the Russian position in the village. This force almost immediately caused the Russians to retreat. Siilasvuo's main forces then moved behind the Russian lines along the Raate highway in order to cut the Russians off from their supply base at Raate itself. Simultaneously, a weaker detachment was to attempt to sever the enemy's lines of support from Juntusranata and block any reinforcements which might try to come to the relief of the trapped Russians. In essence, the plan called for cutting the enemy columns into *mottis* and keeping them isolated from one another until additional troops arrived from Oulu to complete their destruction.

Although there had been little time for preparations and the maps of the area were outdated and partly erroneous, it was clear that the attack had to begin on the 11th since the enemy was persistently attacking in the direction of Haukiperä ferry. If these attacks succeeded, the Russians would be able to encircle the beleagured Finns. Moreover, the weather was worsening as the temperature dipped as low as — 40 degrees Fahrenheit.

Leaving machine gunners to hold

The Finnish 9th Division sets out to attack the Raate-Suomussalmi road

the position south of Suomussalmi, the attack groups moved to their staging areas without coming in contact with the enemy. When they crossed the lake south-east of Suomussalmi; however, they came up against a Russian detachment on the road between Lakes Kuomas and Kuivas. Leaving part of the attack group to build *abatis* at that point to block the enemy, the main force turned toward Suomussalmi. At first, the Finns had difficulty getting a foothold on the road, but once this was accomplished, the advance on the rear of the Russian positions went as planned.

The element of surprise played a large part in the success of this first day's operations. Apparently, the Russians did not guess the strength of the Finnish attack as it approached from the sout-east, because they sent only a small force to block it. This enemy force was quickly destroyed, and the Finns moved on, so that by nightfall they were about a mile and a half from the junction leading to the Haukiperä ferry. In all, they now controlled about three miles of the Raate road. North of the village, the small attack force managed to disrupt Russian communications but was unable to hold the road. After a fierce battle, the group retreated to its staging area.

The following day, the attack was renewed in such cold weather that the trucks had to be left behind, and the men went without a hot meal. Nevertheless, they were in good spirits and moved to their task with vigor. After capturing a Russian position on a small hill which commanded the road, the Finns again advanced.

During the course of the day the Russians sent tanks against their attackers for the first time. Initially, this move caused some consternation in the ranks, but when it was realized that the tanks could not move or fire through the woods, the apprehension subsided. By evening, the Finns had arrived at the junction to the ferry where the Russians had occupied a hill

from which they controlled the road. An assault upon the hill was repulsed during the day, but that night the Russians abandoned the position of their own accord and it was taken over by the Finns. By this time, the Finns had complete control of the area and the road for a distance of about seven and half miles. Without a doubt, the plan was working to perfection, and the Russians were being crowded into *mottis* without realizing what was happening. Of course, they knew nothing about such unconventional tactics and were therefore unprepared to cope with them.

On the 13th, the Finns attacked Suomussalmi village and reached its edge by evening. During the night, they quietly moved into positions close to the front of the Russian lines, in preparation for an attack on the village itself the next morning. In the village the Russians were entrenched in the ruins of buildings, cellars, and dugouts, with tanks guarding the perimeter. Against this formidable obstacle, Siilasvuo proposed to throw his small force, which had no anti-tank guns or artillery to speak of and which was beginning to show signs of exhaustion.

Meanwhile, another attack to the north on Hulkonniemi had succeeded in establishing a foothold, which gave the Finns an opportunity to harass the Russians from the rear. Inspite of heavy enemy attacks and fire, this attack force managed to hold its positions until the 18th, when it was finally forced to retreat. Meanwhile, it helped to relieve the pressure on the forces attacking the Russians from the south-east side of the village.

On the 14th, the Finns again attacked the Russian positions in Suomussalmi but despite furious fighting failed to break through the lines. As the

Above: Finnish officers confer prior to an assault on the village. *Below:* Finnish sharpshooters in action to the south of the village, still held by the Russians

The arrival of anti-tank guns at last provides the answer to the dominance of the Soviet tanks

Finnish forces moved through the outskirts of the village, they were occasionally fired upon from behind by machine gun nests which had not been destroyed. While the main Finnish forces concentrated on the village, another group had moved across the lake north and east of the Russians to keep it under surveillance, fearing that it would be used as a supply route.

By the 18th, Siilasvuo called off the attacks in the area of the village, since they were costing too much in casualties and since the troops were near exhaustion. But by this time the 163rd Division was completely surrounded and broken up into several *mottis*; all that the Finns had to do was to keep it from disengaging until further reinforcements arrived. In the interim, the Finns busily strengthened their positions as best they could, in preparation for further actions.

At about the same time, scouts reported the approach of more enemy troops coming from the direction of Raate and the north. To add to the worry, the 163rd Division was obviously preparing measures to break out of the Finnish snare. Fortunately, reinforcements were also on the way to the Finns, and by the 20th, two batteries and two anti-tank guns had arrived.

With the fresh troops and additional weapons, Siilasvuo ordered his men to the attack once more on the 20th. Again, even with the anti-tank guns, the Finns experienced difficulties with the tanks. These problems were compounded by the fact that the Russians were so well dug in and were defending themselves with the determination of doomed men. As the battle raged, it became clear that the Finns still did not have sufficient strength to deal effectively with the enemy, but at least they were able to keep the Russians pinned down.

On the 21st and 22nd, a small detachment was sent out to destroy a bridge behind the Russians who were being held at the roadblock on the Raate road between Lakes Kuomas and Kuivas. The attempt itself failed, but it produced evidence that the Russians were expecting reinforcements, because they made a surprise attack on the anti-tank group accompanying the attacking force. As yet, however, the Finns were unaware of the magnitude of the approaching threat. Gradually the picture cleared, showing that an entire new division, the 44th, a crack motorized organization from the Moscow military district, was on its way from Raate to extricate the 163rd from

its predicament. Under these circumstances, the Finnish attacking group fell back behind its own lines to await reinforcements.

Only two companies were holding the road against the parts of the 163rd Division held up at Lakes Kuomas and and Kuivas and the advancing 44th Division. The question was whether these troops would be able to hold the line until the destruction of the rest of the 163rd Division was completed and reinforcements could be sent from Suomussalmi. Almost incredibly, these few men did hold the roadblock until help arrived some two weeks later.

Siilasvuo, meanwhile, had regroup-

ed his forces in anticipation of the arrival of the remainder of the 9th Division from Oulu, which was due on 25th December. His plan now called for a main attack to be made from the west and north behind the Russians trapped on Hulkonniemi, while a smaller force assaulted them from the east. Enemy forces in the village itself were to be pinned down by a series of small attacks during the main offensive. If everything went according to plan, the 163rd Division would be cut into successively smaller *mottis*, which would make their destruction inevitable. The attack was set for the morning of 26th December.

All the planning was almost thrown

out of gear, however, by a furious Russian counterattack, supported by bombers and fighters, against all the Finnish positions on the 24th and 25th. Although this attack was contained, it compelled Siilasvuo to postpone his own attack until the 27th, so that his men could rest. In spite of the two weeks of hard combat and the attendant fatigue of the Finns, the attack commenced in the early hours of the 27th. For two days the battle raged. Operations north of the village quickly broke through the Russian front line and cut the enemy into smaller groups; savage counterattacks availed them nothing but more casualties. By the night of the 27th, the Russians were crowded into a small area with few supplies and less hope.

During the first day of the battle,

Left: Russian dead from the 163rd Division. *Below:* A Finnish officer inspects the booty after the virtual destruction of the Russian 163rd Division near Suomussalmi

aerial reconnaissance reported that major preparations by the 44th Division to break through the roadblock and relieve the 163rd were under way. These reports caused considerable anxiety until a new battalion arrived later in the day and was sent to reinforce the roadblock. With great difficulty, the road was held against the Russian attack the next day.

On the 28th, the Finns made a decisive penetration of the Russian southern lines on Hulkonniemi. This development threw the enemy into a panic, and he fled across the ice of Lake Kianta. Another panic set in at Suomussalmi, and soon all but about a third of the division, which was surrounded north of Hulkonniemi, was fleeing across the ice under the protection of their remaining tanks, while the Finns pursued them on skis and strafed them from the air. Only a few small units survived this rout.

The next day the remnants of the 163rd Division were given the same treatment. With a third of the enemy

The Finnish 9th Division, now reinforced, prepares the annihilate the trapped 44th Soviet Division west of Raate

division still to be dealt with, however, Siilasvuo did not feel free to send more than one battalion to the roadblock; nevertheless, it continued to hold. Although trapped, the remaining Russians of the 163rd made a courageous effort to break through their encirclement, but only a few scattered detachments succeeded.

When the day ended, the 163rd Ukrainian Division was, for all practical purposes, completely destroyed. Left on the battlefield were 5,000 dead, innumerable others buried under the snow, and there were 500 prisoners. The booty was impressive and made a welcome addition to the Finnish war effort. It included twenty-five field guns, eleven tanks, 150 trucks, 250 horses, and huge quantities of rifles and ammunition.

Though they had been stretched almost beyond the limits of physical and mental endurance, the Finnish troops were allowed no respite. After a few hours of rest, they returned to the battle, this time against the 44th Division, which was now to feel the effectiveness of *motti* tactics.

Motti tactics entailed a threefold process: reconnaissance and blocking, followed by attack and isolation and then by annihilation. Stage one had been completed while the fighting raged at Suomussalmi. Now, with its column strung out over the twenty miles of road back as far as Raate, the 44th Division offered a prime target for stages two and three. However, the *motti* process was not to be as simple as it sounded, because the Russians were entrenched on both sides of the road to protect themselves from the Finnish patrols, and they were using their tanks to keep their communications open. For a quarter of a mile on either side of the highway they had felled the trees to provide a buffer between themselves and the Finnish

partisans who attacked day and night from the cover of the forests. The Russians did not dare move much beyond their own perimeters, and rarely did their patrols enter the woods. It was remarked at the time that the Russian troops suffered from claustrophobia when they got into a small grove of trees. Because of their lack of reconnaissance, the Russians did not know the size of the attacking force. They apparently believed it to be much larger than it was, since they made no great effort to extricate themselves from the trap. Moreover, since communications between the two enemy divisions had been cut, the commanders of the 44th probably did not know the extent of the disaster which had befallen the 163rd Division.

For the purposes of Siilasvuo's troops, the terrain and conditions were perfect. About two or three miles south of the road was a long lake, which served as a highway on which they could move unobserved into attacking positions along the Russian lines. From the lake, they had only to move through the woods to within striking distance of the

92

Russian positions. Thus, in spite of four feet of snow and the arctic temperatures, the Finns had no difficulty preparing for the attack.

On New Year's Eve, the attack began with a strike against enemy positions just behind the roadblock. The objective was to isolate these forces from those further back as well as to feel the Russians out. On the 2nd, the attack was renewed but ran into stiff resistance, especially from the tanks. Fortunately, the rest of the 9th Division arrived that day, having finished mopping-up operations north of Suomussalmi. Using these additional forces, the Finns were able to complete the isolation of the enemy's forward group from the rest of the column.

On the 5th, a general attack was commenced over the entire length of the enemy column, with the objective of cutting the Russians into manageable *mottis*. Trees were felled and *abatis* constructed across the road with mines and guns to defend them. It was impossible for the tanks to bypass the obstacles because of Finnish firepower, the deep snow, and the dense forests. Tanks thrown against

the *abatis* were destroyed and added to the blockade. By the end of the first day of the general attack, the 44th Division was severed at a number of points so that the individual segments were incapable of mutual support. By the second day, the Russian soldiers were showing signs of nervousness, and when the Finnish attacks began, they fled into the wilderness without any attempt to repel the attackers. Pressing their advantage, the Finns moved inside the Russian positions; by nightfall, they had virtually destroyed every *motti*. The next day the final operations finished off the 44th Division. Only a few scattered detachments escaped to tell the tale.

When stock was taken, the booty was found to include 43 tanks, 50 field guns, 25 anti-tank weapons, 270 trucks, cars, and tractors, 300 machine guns, 6,000 rifles, 32 field kitchens, and 1,170 horses. Enemy casualties could not be reckoned because the bodies were scattered so far and most were buried beneath the snow. The prisoners taken numbered 1,300. Finnish casualties for both Suomussalmi and the Raate road were 900 killed and 1,770 wounded.

The destruction of the 163rd and 44th Russian Divisions was decisive for the enemy's operations in the north. During the rest of the war, no further attempts were made to cut Finland at the waist. Thus, the Finns were able to transfer many of the units from the Arctic to the Karelian front. These victories were the result of a bold and energetic command, which used the troops, the terrain, and the conditions to the best possible advantage. In the annals of warfare, one must look to classical times for parallels to this annihilation of such large numbers by so few.

While the destruction of the Russian divisions at Suomussalmi was going on, the defenders at Kuhmo managed to keep the Red 54th Division at an impasse. After completing operations at Suomussalmi, the Finnish 9th Division was transported to Kuhmo to begin the same process. The first detachments arrived on 26th January. Again, the battle plan was to cut the enemy columns into isolated groups through the use of mobile ski units and hit-and-run operations, thereby creating a constant sense of uncer-

tainty, fear, and depression in the enemy.

As the 9th Division now prepared for the Kuhmo operations, its experiences at Suomussalmi were invaluable. From north of the main highway held by the Russians, the Finns began improvements on a road which would bring them into a position behind the enemy. All this activity went unnoticed by the Russians, since the Finns worked mostly at night. Along the road, they stored supplies and set up insulated tents ready for the time when battle-weary troops would need a warm bed. Some dugouts were also constructed as defensive measures.

On 28th January, the attack began with a small force moving against the enemy groups nearest Kuhmo. The Russians resisted stubbornly, and the attack proved indecisive. But it did permanently stall the Russian advance on Kuhmo itself.

The full attack on the Russian

Below: Some of the 270 trucks abandoned to the Finns. **Right:** Few Russians escaped from the *mottis* on the road to Suomussalmi

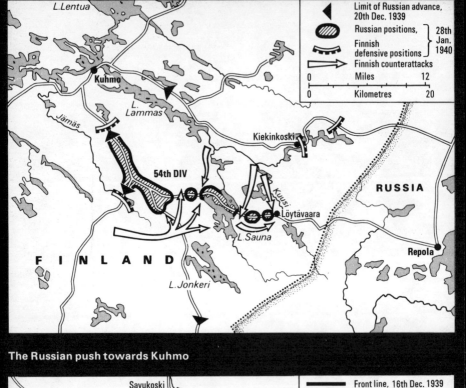

The Russian push towards Kuhmo

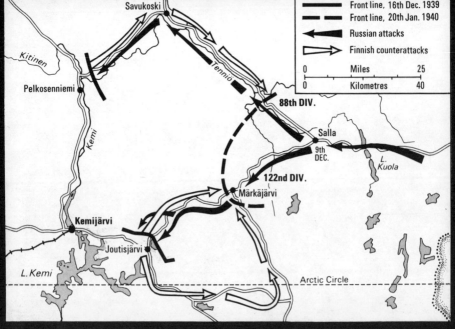

The Russian push towards Kemijärvi

positions behind the roadblock began the next day. One battalion, divided into two groups, closed in from the north, while three battalions, moving in two columns, advanced from the south-east shore of Lake Sauna. Both attacking forces reached the road, but the group from the north was checked before it gained control of its assigned section. Unknowingly, it had stumbled upon the Russian forward command post, whose defenses it could not crack. The two columns from the south-east separated at the road: one battalion followed the road toward the south-east, charged with the mission of blocking the road from that direction; the other two battalions turned north-west, their objective to roll up the Russian positions in that direction. The section of road between these two groups was quickly cleared of enemy troops, and communications between the front and rear sections of the enemy column were severed.

Before long, however, both Finnish groups ran into Russian-built bunkers which were staunchly defended by their occupants. In addition, Russian tanks appeared, causing complica-

Finnish troops crawl past the body of a Russian soldier during an attack on an enemy bunker

tions for the Finns. This time, however the Finns used captured Russian anti-tank guns against the tanks. The worst problem turned out to be the log bunkers, because they were almost impervious to the fire from grenade launchers, and there were not enough cannons available to smash them. The Finns did use the anti-tank guns against weak points in the bunkers, but this tactic proved only partially successful. It was thus impossible to smash the Russian positions completely.

In spite of these setbacks, the Finns succeeded during the next few days in chopping the Russian column into ten *mottis* along sixteen miles of highway. This success still left the Finns with some serious problems. The main difficulty was that the new Finnish supply road from the north came to an end at a point between two *mottis* which were only a half mile apart. In early February, the Russians managed to cut the supply road and hold it for a few days and only after

97

two strenuous counterattacks were the Finns able to open the road again. At the same time, the Russians stubbornly resisted efforts to squeeze them into more concentrated positions to relieve the pressure on the Finnish forces operating on the road between the two *mottis*. Success finally came on 25th February, when the eastern *motti* gave way, and the 27th, when the western section gave way. However, these two large *mottis* were never completely annihilated, although they suffered heavy losses.

The Finns were not as successful in their operations at Kuhmo as they had been at Suomussalmi, but it should be remembered that the Russians were far less passive at Kuhmo. Food, forage, ammunition, and gasoline were dropped from the air to the trapped column, while relief expeditions from their 23rd Division, supported by tanks and artillery, remained a constant threat to the Finnish operations, requiring a great deal of their time and energy to fend them off. Without planes to command the air and enough artillery to smash

the bunkers, the Finns could not really accomplish their overall objectives. Moreover, the difficulty in getting supplies was as bad for the Finns as it was for the Russians.

During February, the Finnish forces withstood several strenuous counterattacks by the Russians but still managed to keep the *mottis* isolated. Fortunately, on these occasions the enemy again failed to coordinate his efforts. For example, in one of the attacks, the enemy tanks managed to break through the Finnish lines, but instead of splitting up in two groups and attacking in two directions simultaneously, the whole tank force went in one direction. Thus, the Finns were able to move in quickly behind them and force their withdrawal. This and other efforts to break out of the encirclement resulted in heavy losses for the Russians.

In a desperate bid to meet the Finns on their own footing, the Russians sent a ski brigade from the northern road through the forests, intending to spring their trapped compatriots loose. According to Khruschev, these

were some of the best skiers the Soviet Union had to offer, and well they might have been – on the Russian plains; when it came to the forests of Finland, however, their expertise was found wanting. In the forests, they came in contact on 11th February with a Finnish patrol and lost many men in the ensuing skirmish, including fifty captured. Disregarding this reversal, the ski brigade pushed on through the woods toward the Finnish positions at Kiekinkoski, on the north road leading to Kuhmo. For a time thereafter they disappeared out of sight, but they managed to reach the area of the new Finnish supply road by the 14th. For a time, they were able to cut the road, because the only forces the Finns had in the area were supply troops and men resting from their exertions at the front. Too weak to stop the Russians with an attempted counterattack, the rearline troops could do little other than to let the Russians settle into their quarters.

But a reinforced Finnish ski company was soon on the enemy's trail. Coming upon the Russians, the ad-

vance group of Finns attacked before the rest of the company arrived, even though the enemy appeared to be far superior in manpower. This superiority was mitigated by the fact that the Russians' semi-automatic rifles would not function in the extreme cold because, as was learned later, they had not cleaned the grease from the weapons carefully enough. When their rifles did not fire, the Russians would leap up and try to bayonet or even to seize the Finns with their bare hands. During the course of the battle, however, the Finns suddenly discovered that a Russian group had moved in behind them. Under the circumstances, the Finns found themselves precariously holding their position through the night while waiting for the rest of the company.

When the rest of the Finns arrived, the Russian ski brigade was forced to disengage. Their route to their beleagured compatriots blocked, part of the Russian brigade moved northwest, only to be turned back. Another part of the group went north, where it was attacked from two sides. The harried Russians now fled to the east, seeking an escape. About 100 got lost and were killed. The main force remained in the Finnish bunkers, where it met its destruction. Throwing hand grenades and shouting for the Russians to surrender, the Finns made an all-out attack upon the bunkers. When this failed, the bunkers were set ablaze, but still the enemy refused to surrender, trying instead to break through the Finnish lines. Most of the Russians died in the attempt. When it was all over, there were over 300 dead in front of the bunkers and forty bodies in the burnt out ruins. Only four men surrendered. When a final count was taken, almost 1,500 dead Russian skiers were found in the Finnish forests. A friend of the

Russian ski-troops advance to engage the Finns south of Kuhmo with disastrous results to themselves

author, Colonel A K Marttinen, who was Chief of Staff for Siilasvuo at the time, has provided an interesting footnote to this episode: he has stated that when the Russian skis were collected, they were found to be of such poor quality as to be useful only for firewood.

Towards the end of the month, the Russians of the 44th made a great effort to extricate themselves from their predicament. Increasingly heavy artillery fire was directed at the Finnish positions at Kuusijoki. After a series of battles, the Finns withdrew from the area and used the troops to reinforce the *motti* at Löytävaara. Here, the Russians made several attempts to break out but were driven back every time, and the situation remained unchanged until the end of the war.

At the same time, an attempt was made to complete the destruction of the *motti* near Lake Sauna. Here, too,

the war ended before the operation was completed, although one part of the enemy forces was destroyed. The Finnish commanders in the area believed that had the war lasted a day or two more, the whole *motti* would have been annihilated.

Although the battles at Kuhmo ended without the total triumph that was achieved at Suomussalmi, there can be no doubt that the Russians had suffered a stinging defeat. But the Finns also suffered proportionately more at Kuhmo than in any other sector, since the loss of officers was greater than usual in these assaults, where personal example very often determined the outcome.

Further north, above the Arctic Circle, at Salla and Petsamo, the Russian invasion was also halted. At Salla, two enemy divisions had driven out the one battalion of defenders from the village on 9th December. This success opened the road to Kemijärvi and Pelkosenniemi and cleared the way for an advance toward the north-west and south-west, where it might be possible for these divisions to join up with the invading

Left : Russian prisoners. *Below :*
Finnish ski-troops on the move near Petsamo where the Russian invasion was halted on the northern front

columns from Petsamo and Suomus-salmi and Kuhmo.

By the 16th, the Russians were only about fourteen miles from Kemijärvi and were expected to move in that direction. Instead, a regiment reinforced by tanks and a reconnaissance battalion was detached from the two divisions at Salla and began to move toward Savukosi and Pelkosenniemi. Meanwhile, the meager Finnish forces had been reinforced by a relief battalion. With these few troops, the Finns took the initiative on the 18th and decided the issue by a flank attack. The Russians fled back to Salla in a blind panic, leaving behind ten tanks, forty trucks, and miscellaneous arms and ammunition.

After that, the enemy dug in at Salla, and the front was quiet for a month. There were two minor assaults on the Red positions on the Salla-Kemijärvi road on 2nd and 3rd January, but these skirmishes produced no significant results. The Russians were cleared from some parts of the road after losing some 200 men. By this time, the Finnish soldiers were so exhausted that further attacks were impossible. Falling back on guerrilla tactics, the Finns now proceeded to harass the Russians in the rear, disrupting their lines of communication, their road traffic and destroying the bridges. In the face of these torments, the Russians dug in more deeply, building bunkers while their tanks patroled the road along with some ski troops.

From mid-January, the Finns once again took the offensive. This attack succeeded in forcing the Russians to retreat to stronger positions at Märkäjärvi, to the south-west of Salla, where they remained until the end of the war. Later, a Russian force tried to expel a couple of weak Finnish battalions from their position on the Salla-Pelkosenniemi road but were themselves driven out.

On 26th February, a Swedish volunteer group arrived and was placed in charge of containing the Russians, while the Finnish battalions were transferred to the battlefield at Viipuri. Although the Finns had been too weak numerically to employ *motti* tactics effectively at Salla as had been done at Suomussalmi, they had withstood an overwhelming attack and held their ground. No more could be expected of them.

An account of operations above the Arctic Circle would be incomplete without a brief description of the actions in the Petsamo area. The port at Petsamo is ice-free but it lies some 250 miles from the nearest railroad and is only connected to southern Finland by a narrow highway. Hence, it was so far removed from the main theater of the war as to be quite neglected during the conflict. For the Russians, of course, with their rail connections to Murmansk and their Arctic Fleet in the waters around Petsamo, an invasion of the area was quite feasible. Russian interest in the area stemmed in large part from the nickel mines in the area, which were among the richest in Europe.

When the invasion began, the Finns had only one company reinforced by an artillery battery, to defend the whole region against a Russian division. The artillery pieces dated from 1887. What few reserves were available were located in several hamlets. At the outbreak of war, the Russians immediately occupied the Fisherman's Peninsula and then advanced south in three columns, driving everything before them. However, the extremely cold weather and Finnish guerrilla tactics stalled the advance. The Russians then dug in, with their tanks defending the perimeter of their defenses. By 18th January the front was stabilized at Nautsi, where it remained until the end of the war.

February offensive

After suffering staggering defeats on the Karelian Isthmus during December, the Russians remained relatively inactive throughout January, although it had been expected that they would immediately throw everything they had into a new attack in order to restore their shattered prestige. Instead, they spent the month transporting vast quantities of artillery, ammunition, and equipment, along with several new divisions, into their rear positions. At the same time, they extended and improved their communications network on the Isthmus. A further reason for the quiet was that a change of command took place after the initial defeats. K E Voroshilov, Commissar for Defense, was replaced by Marshal Semyon Timoshenko, who was also appointed Commander-in-Chief of the Red forces operating on the Isthmus. Timoshenko was a thorough and systematic commander who did not expend his energies and efforts uselessly. It was also true that the Soviet strategists were probably anticipating a breakthrough north of Lake Lagoda, which would have meant the encirclement of the Finnish forces on the Isthmus and the severing of the rail connections with Sweden.

During January the Russians used reconnoitering expeditions and aerial balloons to pinpoint Finnish artillery

Russian troops pass through the tank-traps of the Mannerheim Line

emplacements and bunkers; the information they gathered improved the accuracy of their artillery greatly. Throughout the month, the Finnish positions were subjected to incessant bombardments from the ground and air. Behind the lines, the Russian troops underwent intensive training for the attack to come; part of this training included assaults on various sectors of the Finnish lines. These practice attacks were clearly better organized than those of December: only after an intensive bombardment to soften up the Finnish positions did the infantry go in and then only in close cooperation with armored units.

For the Finnish troops, the waiting period was demoralizing, not only because of the uncertainty but also because of the constant artillery and air bombardments. Finnish field communications were virtually destroyed, many of the concrete pillboxes were ground to powder, and during the daylight a man alone could not venture out even behind the lines because of the aerial attacks. As the month passed, it became increasingly necessary to conduct all movements and activities at night; fires in the tents and bunkers had to be extinguished at dawn in spite of temperatures as low as − 22 degrees Fahrenheit. Finnish artillery operations were seriously curtailed at the same time.

On both sides, regrouping and reorganization was effected during the waiting period. The Finns withdrew the 5th Division from the line and replaced it with the 6th, which was now renamed the 3rd Division. To the 5th Division were attached several independent units, and this force became the main reserve. The 21st Division was combined with the 1st Division and placed in positions on the eastern end of the Isthmus as the reserve of the Commander-in-Chief. On the Russian side, Timoshenko divided his forces on the Isthmus into the Seventh and Thirteenth Armies.

Captured Russian trench mortar bombs

Marshal G Stern, new commander of the Russian Army Group North

In the north, the Russian Ninth, Fourteenth and Eighteenth Armies were combined into one army group under the command of Marshal Stern.

When the Russian attack began on 1st February, it was concentrated mainly on the western side of the Isthmus, especially against the defenses in the Summa sector. At the time, the opposing forces were deployed as follows: from the coast of the Gulf of Finland to Suokanta, the Finnish 4th Division faced three Russian divisions: the 43rd, the 138th, and the 70th; from Suokanta to the railroad, the 3rd Division opposed the enemy's 123rd and 90th Divisions and the 40th Tank Brigade; from the railroad to Lake Muola, the Finnish 1st Division confronted the Red 24th Division; from Lake Muola to Vuoksi, the 2nd Division held the line against the Soviet 136th and 142nd Divisions; the Finnish 8th Division held positions from Vuoksi to Sakkola gainst the Red 4th Division, but there were probably other Soviet contingents involved there as well; the 7th Division held the sector from Sakkola to Lake Ladoga against the 49th and

The Ilyushin Il-4 (DB-3). Russia's standard medium bomber throughout the Second World War. It was also very successful as a torpedo bomber. Its most noteworthy feature was its excellent range. The following specification refers to the DB-3F, a more streamlined version. *Engines*: two M-8 radials, 1,100-hp each. *Armament*: three 7.62mm machine guns and up to 4,400 lbs of bombs or one 18-inch torpedo. *Speed*: 265 mph at 20,000 feet. *Ceiling*: 30,700 feet. *Range*: 2,500 miles. *Weight loaded*: 20,600 lbs. *Span*: 70 feet 2 inches. *Length*: 47 feet 6 inches. *Crew*: four.

The Tupolev ANT-6 (TB-3). Russia's main bomber in the early 1930s. Though obsolete by 1939 it was used in the Second World War as a transport and paratroop aircraft after serving in its original form in the Winter War. *Engines*: four AM-34 inlines, 830-hp each. *Armament*: eight 7.62mm machine guns and up to 6,600 lbs of bombs. *Speed*: 155 mph. *Ceiling*: 16,400 feet. *Range*: 1,245 (with 3,300-lb bomb load). *Weight loaded*: 39,683 lbs. *Span*: 132 feet 10½ inches. *Length*: 80 feet 0½ inches. *Crew*: eight.

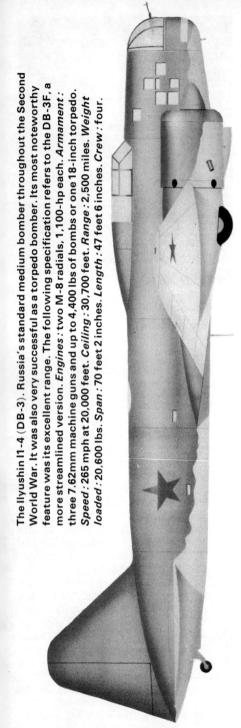

150th Soviet Divisions. Behind the lines, the Russians had as reserves one army tank corps and at least three infantry divisions. Against these forces, the Finns were able to raise only the 5th and 21st Divisions as strategic reserves.

In the early hours of 1st February, the heaviest artillery barrage up until that time began; overhead, some 500 bombers also came into the attack. Finnish air reconnaissance reported that the Russians had 104 batteries in action, or about 400 field guns. The Russians were so sure that the Finnish Air Force and artillery could not harm them that they did not even bother to camouflage their firing positions.

At noon, the tanks moved toward the Finnish lines, pushing rollers in front of them to detonate mines and towing armored sleighs filled with infantry. Experience had apparently taught the Russians to utilize the inherent versatility of the tank more effectively. They also used flame-throwers for the first time. Other infantry followed behind the tanks on foot, concealed behind smoke-screens and armored shields.

In this attack, the enemy tanks operated more cautiously than earlier; they did not attempt deep penetrations of the Finnish lines but concentrated their efforts on isolating the concrete bunkers and machine gun nests and blocking up the apertures through which the Finns fired. They paid particular attention to the Finnish tank traps and barbed wire entanglements, seeking to destroy them. Already, the day before, paratroopers had been dropped behind the Finnish lines for the same purpose. In one sector, the Finns fought an airborne unit throughout the first day of the battle but no extensive use of paratroopers was made during the Winter War.

All that day and into the night, the battle raged unabated. Although the Russians received a constant supply of replacements for the fallen, the attacks were repulsed all along the line. That the Finnish positions had taken a beating, however, there could

Finns evacuate an emplacement during the Russian drive towards Viipuri

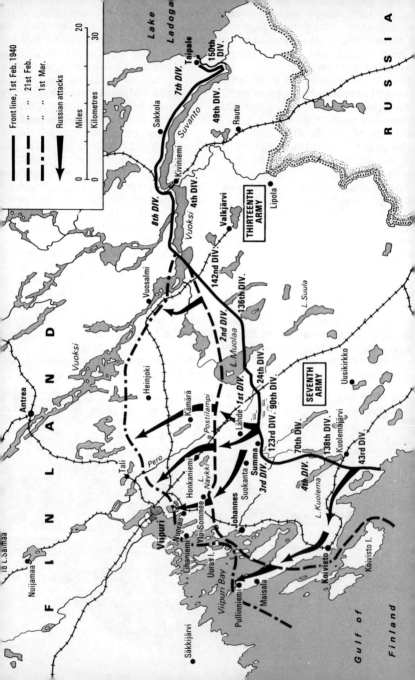

be no doubt. Many of the concrete bunkers were damaged almost beyond repair; artillery emplacements were ruined and machine gun nests destroyed in many places. Repair work on these went on throughout the night in spite of almost continuous bombardment, which was directed especially at the front lines but also at random on the roads in the rear.

This battle was only the curtain raiser for the attacks to follow. There were a few days of relative calm, during which minor probing actions were undertaken, but they were easily repulsed. On the 5th, however, the enemy moved to the attack and again concentrated his main efforts on the Summa sector. Once more, a continuous cannonade during the night preceded the attack. When the attack got under way, it came with full force, but the Finns drove the invaders back. Fourteen tanks were left on the field.

On the 6th, the attack became general all along the front but with the main thrust still aimed at Summa. For the next five days, the Finns took everything the Russians had.

Bombed from the air, bombarded by artillery day and night, and under continuous attack by the infantry during the day, the Finns held their positions with grim determination. During one twenty-four-hour period, the Russians fired as many as 300,000 shells on the Finnish lines.

Unable to crack the Summa defenses, on the 11th the Russians shifted their main efforts to the Lähde sector, further to the east of Summa. Simultaneously, intensive assaults began all across the Isthmus and also across the ice of the Gulf of Finland and Lake Ladoga. The latter were an attempt to roll up the Finnish defenses from the ends. Several dents were made in the line, but with the aid of local reserves the gaps were quickly closed. The use of these local units, however, had reduced the Finnish command to reliance upon the 5th and 21st Divisions – the last of its reserves.

Finnish troops manhandle an anti-tank gun into a hastily constructed bunker in an attempt to halt the Russian offensive

It was at Lähde that the worst attacks occurred. There, the Russians had concentrated so much heavy artillery that the bunkers and machine gun nests were pulverized. By 1 pm, the forwardmost of the bunkers were seized by the enemy, and reinforcements had to be requested from the 5th Division. Later in the afternoon, two Bofors field guns from the 5th Division arrived but no troops. By 7.30 that evening, the enemy tanks and infantry poured into the Finnish positions and penetrated about a mile, to the rear positions. At the same time, the succeeding waves of attackers began to roll up the Finnish defenses from the sides of the breach. Between the enemy and Viipuri stood only a few weak reserves of II Army Corps.

The onslaught continued into the night without a break. An attempted counterattack that night by the defenders at Lähde failed for lack of reinforcments. Not until the next day were reserves able to get to the zone, but even these proved inadequate as only one regiment was available. The rest of the reserve units had to be diverted to the Summa sector to support the wavering line there. Another breach was made in the line north-east of Merkki that night and the next day, and the enemy began moving eastwards. This development was to have serious ramifications later, as it knocked out the cornerstone of the Finnish counterattack the next day.

Fortunately, the rest of the line was still holding when night fell on the 11th. But the strain on the front line troops was beginning to take its toll. The 3rd Division, which been on the line for a month, was so exhausted that its men could hardly keep their

eyes open, even in the face of oncoming tanks. The division was therefore relieved by the 5th Division on the 13th, which meant that there were no strategic reserves at all behind the Summa section and that there would not be any for a week or so, until the men of the 3rd Division were rested.

On the 13th, the Russians sent in fresh troops to widen the gap in the Lähde front, where the Finns had already begun their counterattack that morning. Some of the breach was closed, but since there were no more reserves available, the gains were lost again by that night. One factor complicating the Finnish operation was the presence of Russian ski troops, who were difficult to locate and who also served to confuse the battle.

In the breach itself, the Russians concentrated so many troops and came on so fast that the defenders near Merkki were overrun in their bunkers as the enemy began to roll up the defenses from the sides. Although the Russians suffered terrible losses, they continued to storm the sector with tanks and infantry until by late afternoon the bunkers were useless. On the east side, the line was ripped open, and the Russian infantry, led by fifty tanks, poured through the hole. The Finns threw in the last battalion of reserves but against the tanks and overwhelming numbers of Russians, they were virtually helpless.

The rupture of the Finnish lines forced the Finns to abort their counterattack and to retreat to positions north of Lake Summa. In that sector, the Russians had greatly strengthened and broadened their attack. It was clear that the battle was decidedly in the enemy's favour. Even the heavy howitzers and troop vehicles in the area had been lost. Although the howitzers were old, having seen service in the Russo-Japanese War, their loss was serious for the Finns.

A member of Finland's Defense Corps, a battalion of which was dispatched from Viipuri

had only a few well fortified points.

Meanwhile, reserves were being scraped up from every possible source. Even the navy was called upon to send two regiments to the front near Summa. The 62nd Infantry Regiment from the 21st Division near Taipale was ordered to the western end of the Isthmus on the 13th. But, because of bombing raids, these troops, travelling in open cars in – 22 degrees Fahrenheit (– 30 degrees Centigrade) temperatures, were delayed on the railroad and did not arrive until the 14th. A battalion of Defense Corps, made up almost entirely of young boys, had been assembled in Viipuri and was on its way to the front in automobiles, but it did not arrive until after the withdrawal. Later, the 23rd Division, recently dispatched to the Kollaa front, was recalled to the Isthmus. While the Russians were wielding divisions, the Finns were manipulating battalions.

On the 15th, the enemy attacks continued in the Lähde sector; the Russians quickly overran the remaining defenses and then moved north. As the situation deteriorated during the day and another breach was made in the lines on the Kämärä road, it was clear that a full-scale retreat from the coast to Lake Muola was necessary. At 3.30 pm, the order to withdraw was given.

Fortunately, the Russians did not launch any major attacks during the next few days, which permitted the Finns to reach their new positions in fairly good order. Nevertheless, the road to Viipuri was now open to the enemy. Haunted by this grim reality, the Finnish commanders pondered the question uppermost in their minds; how long could their weary men hold the new positions? Whatever the gravity of the situation in the center of the line, however, the extremities of it had held, and every attempt by the enemy to envelop the Finnish defenses from the ends had been foiled. On the shore of the Gulf of Finland, the coastal batteries, especi-

During the night, the Russians forced their way deeper into the Finnish lines, until they were some two miles behind the main positions. At this point, the Russian infantry in the breach was not yet strong enough to capitalize on the situation, even with the support of the tanks. On the other hand, the Finns did not have the strength to drive them out. On the 14th, the Russians expanded the breach at Lähde and threatened to roll up the entire Summa defense line. The troops in the area immediately threatened were withdrawn to secondary positions some distance to the rear.

There was no question that the enemy would extend the bulge in the line the next day, and the Finnish commanders were faced with the difficult decision of whether to order a general retreat to the secondary line or not. Mannerheim drove to the front on the 14th for consultations with his field commanders; after much discussion, it was decided to withdraw all the troops on the western end of the Isthmus to the secondary line, even though these positions

ally at Koivisto, had proved their worth, driving the Russians back across the ice. Now, even these positions had to be abandoned during the next few days.

The withdrawal presented some difficult problems, since much of it had to be carried out during daylight, thus exposing the retreating men to air raids and tank attacks. But by the 18th, the majority of the troops were in their new positions. Only Koivisto and its surrounding islands were still manned, and an additional regiment was sent to reinforce the the troops already there, since the batteries on Koivisto were important for the protection of the right wing of the Finnish line during the withdrawal. On the 21st, the troops were withdrawn from Koivisto. The defense line then ran from Lasi Island in Viipuri Bay almost due east to the railroad, where it swung south-east to the north end of Lake Muola and from there to the Vuoksi Waterway.

It was the responsibility of the 4th Division to defend the sector nearest the coast, which proved to be the most critical in the coming days.

Already on the night of the 17th, the enemy made contact with the new positions. In the attack the next day, the Russians effected a minor breakthrough at Ylä-Sommee, a short distance inland, which enabled them to occupy a few stone buildings, from which it proved difficult to dislodge them. At this village, as at Summa, the tank obstacles had been located too far from the firing line to be truly effective.

For two days, the 10th Infantry Regiment withstood the full force of the enemy onslaught, which was accompanied by extremely accurate fire. As a result, the regiment suffered heavy casualties and had to be relieved on the 20th. Its successors suffered equally heavy losses, since the Russians hammered continuously at the positions in the village. Finally, a hole was punched in the line just east of the village, but the defenders, in spite of their exhaustion, rallied and drove the Russians back.

Finns are again forced to evacuate their positions in the face of overwhelming Soviet armor and men

Russian bombers attack Viipuri during the Red Army's push towards the town

On the coast, the area to be defended was extensive because of the islands and inlets which had to be kept under surveillance, if not actively defended. During the first few days of the retreat only the 12th Infantry Regiment and the coastal batteries held the whole area. When the Russians commenced operations along the coast on the 18th, they overran several key points and forced the Finns to withdraw to Pullinniemi and Maisala the following day. For some time, these positions were held in spite of furious attacks and rather shaky communications with the main forces. On the other hand, on Koivisto Island, the Finnish troops were virtually isolated, had little or no communication with the mainland, and were threatened with a worse situation if Pullinniemi fell. As the situation deteriorated on the mainland and the Russians obtained positions where they could bring the east side of the island under fire, it was evident that the situation was more than one regiment could handle. On 22nd February, Koivisto Island

was abandoned after all the shells had been fired, the guns spiked and the defense installations destroyed. Carrying what they could, the defenders began a twenty-five mile trek across the ice of Viipuri Bay to Säkkijärvi, where they arrived the next day. For once the gods of war smiled on the weary Finnish troops: as they started out past the enemy's flank, a heavy snow storm began, concealing them from observation.

Lasi Island came under Soviet attack on the morning of the 23rd and was captured before noon. This event threatened the rear of the entire secondary line because it opened the road to Lihaniemi and Viipuri Bay. Because the island was so important to the Finnish defense system, an attempt was made to recapture it that evening, but without success, although the Finns managed to hold the north side of the island for a time.

Not only was the secondary line menaced from its west end but it was also threatened from the east, where the Russians had almost immediately broken through the positions held by the 5th and 23rd Divisions. The breach occurred in an area dominated by

Finnish armor also suffers from the
difficult terrain.

small hills and swamps, between the main road to Viipuri and the railroad. On the 17th, the first dent was made at Postilampi but was quickly rectified, albeit with some difficulty. Another penetration occurred a bit later on the east shore of Lake Näykki. Step by step, the Russians advanced against stiff Finnish resistance, boring an ever larger hole in the line. By 23rd February, the enemy was almost in the open and ready for a run toward Viipuri.

By this time, there was growing concern among the commanders at the front that the secondary positions could not be held for much longer. They submitted their views to Mannerheim on the 18th, but he ordered them to hold the line as long as possible. This response caused some anger among the commanders, but the Marshal had not told them that peace feelers were out and the longer the line held, the better the chances for reasonable terms. Despite their irritation, the commanders followed orders, and the line was held for another ten days.

On 25th February, the Russians completed the breach at Honkaniemi along the railroad and were in position to move on Viipuri and to encircle the Finns from behind. The next day the Finns attempted to counterattack with fifteen Vickers tanks, which had been purchased before the war but had only now received their armaments. The appearance of tanks coming from behind caused a great deal of confusion, and in some instances, panic, among the Finnish rear positions and in the supply traffic on the road. Moreover, the attack was only partially successful, since the tanks had difficulty in the snow and were too light for combat with the Russian twenty-eight-ton tanks. Only half of the Finnish tanks returned to their base. This event signalled the end of the secondary line. On the 27th, the troops were ordered to retreat to the rear lines just outside Viipuri. This line ran around Viipuri to Tali, from where it extended to Vuosalmi on the Vuoksi Waterway.

In order to facilitate the defense of Viipuri and to alleviate some of the burden on the commander of II Army Corps, Mannerheim divided the Corps into the I and II Army Corps. I Corps consisted of the 1st and 2nd Divisions, which held the line from the railroad to the Vuoksi Waterway. II Army Corps, comprised of the 3rd, 4th, 5th, and 23rd Divisions, was to concentrate its efforts on the defense of Viipuri.

With these changes in the command organization and the strong defensive positions that Viipuri offered, the Finnish High Command hoped to hold the enemy at bay until the peace negotiators had completed their task.

Finnish Vickers 6-ton tanks were found inadequate against the Russian armor

The possibilities for holding the lines around Viipuri were much better than those of the secondary positions, since the former were more permanent and since civilians had worked throughout the war to build more positions and reinforce those already in existence. In the face of the new fortifications and the ancient moats and stone fortifications, as well as better-constructed tank traps, the enemy would find it difficult to storm the city.

The retreat to the rear positions was in no sense a rout or even, for that matter, a hasty withdrawal, in spite of the Russians' close pursuit. It was carried out in orderly, gradual steps, and the Russians paid dearly for every foot of ground they gained. On the shore of the Bay at Lihaniemi, the systematic withdrawal was endangered by strong enemy pressure, but even here the rear guard did its duty without flinching. Already on 29th February, however, the Russians made contact with the outposts of the rear line at Nuoraa and on 1st March arrived in front of the 3rd Division's right wing. To the east of the 3rd Division, the 5th Division was withdrawn in good order but was forced to move more quickly than planned when the enemy broke through the lines held by the 23rd Division to its left. The Russian penetration of the 23rd's position on the 28th was the result of a massive tank attack, which carried the enemy almost to the rear positions by 1st March. Artillery fire from the guns captured at Suomussalmi finally halted the Russian advance at Ukonmäki. By the 1st, the withdrawal was completed, and the stage was set for the final act of the war.

The final act

No respite was in store for the exhausted men as they took up their new positions around Viipuri. Even as the last of the rear guard pulled back, the enemy was hammering on the rear positions. By this time serious peace discussions were in progress between Helsinki and Moscow via Stockholm; from information received, it was clear that the Kremlin was determined to take as much territory from Finland as possible. For this reason, the battle for Viipuri took on added importance to both sides, accounting for the savage assaults II Army Corps and Coast Group were subjected to during the final days of the war.

Immediately in front of the city itself, the 3rd and 5th Divisions held a line from Käremäenlahti to Tammisuo. In this sector, the Russians drove a wedge in the line at Huhtiala on 2nd March. They followed up this success the next day with a push that drove all the Finnish lookouts from their forward positions back behind their main positions, except at Tammisuo, where a few Finns continued to hold a small hill. On 4th March, the enemy attacked all along the front without success; however, by that evening there were signs that the line might buckle, and a regiment had to be sent in from the 3rd Division's reserves. Another of the 3rd's reserve

The castle at Viipuri, key to the interior of Finland

battalions had to be sent to the north shore of Viipuri Bay to support the forces fighting to keep the Russians from making a landing there.

The Russians continued to storm the 3rd Division's defenses on the 5th, threatening for a moment to smash the line at Lintumus. At Tammisuo, two successive tank assaults were repulsed. During the following day, there was only slight activity on the whole sector, although the artillery barrages continued with the same intensity and a minor assault at Lintumus had to be fought off. On the 7th, a small breach was made at Huhtiala; since the Finns were unable to seal off this gap, the matter was critical by the 8th. Almost all the reserves available to II Army Corps had been sent into combat, even the supply and construction units. Every available reserve unit from I Army Corps was on its way to the Viipuri area but could still not be expected for many hours.

On the 10th, in order to conserve the strength of the forces, the Isthmus Army Command decided that the 3rd Division's line should be shortened by a withdrawal to the south edge of Viipuri. Orders for the withdrawal were suspended, however, and the front remained where it was. For their part, the Russians did not ease the pressure, but increased it. On the 11th, two more punctures were made in the 3rd Division's sector and permission was given by the Isthmus Command for the troops to withdraw to the edge of the city. At this point, Mannerheim intervened and ordered the 3rd to hold the line where it was, at least until the following evening, because of foreign policy. Not knowing what was going on, the front line commanders were incensed but grimly carried out their orders.

During the night of 11th March, the Russians broke through the Finnish lines between Kesämaa and Porkka Island, south-west of the city at the

Below: Finnish artillery desperately try to prevent the encirclement of the town. *Right:* Gunners of the Finnish 5th Division hold back the enemy from Viipuri

point where the right wing of the 3rd Division touched the left wing of the forces defending the Bay. This rupture posed such a threat to the whole defense system that Öhquist, Commander of II Army Corps, considered ordering a retreat. But since Mannerheim's order still stood, an incomplete battalion was found and sent to shore up the sagging line, which then held.

In the morning, the enemy commenced the heaviest attack yet all along the lines of the 3rd and 5th Divisions. By nightfall, a number of large gaps had been made in the Finnish lines between Karjala and Tammisuo, but there was no possibility of a counterattack: the exhausted men were barely able to hold the positions. At the point of the largest rupture, near Tammisuo, the Russians proceeded to expand the gap toward the west and southwest, threatening to engulf the 3rd Division. Again, Öhquist requested permission to pull all his forces back to the edge of Viipuri but was allowed to withdraw only the 3rd Division as far as Patterimäki. When the retreat got under way, the Russians followed tight behind, but the Finns were able to set the southern outskirts of the city ablaze to slow the enemy down.

Later that night, the 5th Division managed to get the situation at Tammisuo under control, isolating the enemy tanks from their infantry. This success presented the Finns with a good possibility of putting the Russians in a sack and drawing it closed. Nevertheless, the situation was critical, since there was no guarantee that the sack would remain closed when operations resumed the next day. After the usual morning attacks began and were repulsed the next day, however, the guns were silenced, and peace returned, much to the surprise of defenders and attackers.

While the 3rd and 5th Divisions had been fighting in front of Viipuri, the Finnish 23rd Division held the line to the east, from Tali to Vuosalmi on the Vuoksi Waterway. The retreat to the rear positions on the east end of the line had been made in good order, with fewer enemy attacks in the rear of the withdrawing troops. It was not until 3rd March that the first significant Russian contact with the new position was made in the area of Tali, although further east the Soviet troops appeared before the Finnish lines at Mustalahti somewhat earlier. On the 4th, the enemy attacked and was repelled with great difficulty. The next day the Red troops penetrated the line south-west of Tali.

During the 6th, the Red forces sought to deepen their penetration, at the same time piercing another hole in the lines just to the right of the first breach. The Finns tried to flood the area, but the scheme backfired, since the water froze solid in short order; where it rose to the level of the tank traps, it facilitated the advance of the enemy's tanks. At the same time, the 23rd Division found itself by the transfer of a battalion from its ranks to the north shore of Viipuri Bay.

From the 8th onward, the Russians hammered at the Finnish positions incessantly until the very last minute of the war. During the 8th, the forward positions around Tali were entirely lost and the men withdrawn to a rear line immediately in front of the village. A counterattack was made a few hours later, but it accomplished nothing and cost a large number of casualties. During the night, the Russians threw fresh troops into the battle on the western part of the Tali positions, thus massing themselves all around the village. The sheer number of Russian troops occasioned the only real panic II Army Corps had experienced in the war. Somehow or other, word got about that the Russian tanks had burst through the lines. This could not have been so, since the tanks would have had to cross the flooding Pero River without

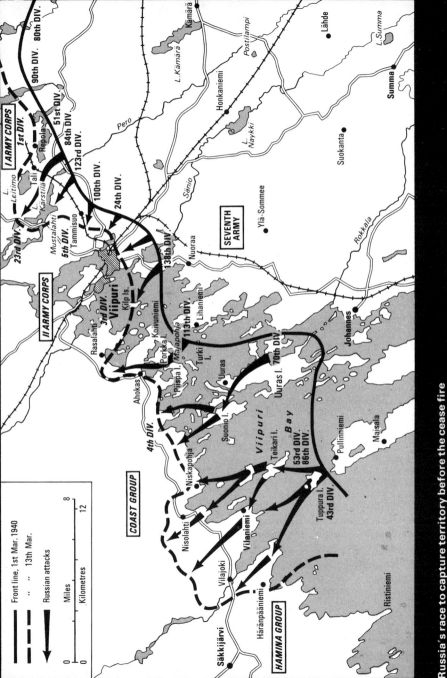

Russia's race to capture territory before the cease fire

Front line, 1st Mar. 1940
,, ,, 13th Mar.
Russian attacks

Miles
0   8
Kilometres
0   12

I ARMY CORPS
80th DIV.
90th DIV.
51st DIV.
84th DIV.
123rd DIV.
1st DIV.
100th DIV.
24th DIV.
23rd DIV.
5th DIV.
138th DIV.
3rd DIV.
113th DIV.
70th DIV.
4th DIV.
53rd DIV.
86th DIV.
43rd DIV.

II ARMY CORPS

SEVENTH ARMY

COAST GROUP

HAMINA GROUP

Kämärä
Lähde
L. Summa
Summa
Postilampi
L. Kämärä
Honkaniemi
Suokanta
Pero
L. Näykki
Sainio
Ylä-Sommee
Rokkala
L. Leitimo
Repola
Tali
Karstila
Mustasuo
Tammisuo
Nuoraa
Nuoraa
Viipuri
Kilp. Is.
Rasalahti
Koivuniemi
Porkka
Piispa I.
Majapohja
Turki I.
Lihaniemi
Uuras
Uuras I.
Johannes
Ahokas
Suonio I.
V i i p u r i   B a y
Teikari I.
Pullinniemi
Maisala
Niskapohja
Nisolahti
Vilajoki
Vilaniemi
Tuppura I.
Ristiniemi
Häränpääniemi
Säkkijärvi

The 23rd Division manages to counter-attack in spite of the Russian advance

any prior preparations; nevertheless, a battalion on the line panicked and fled. Other troops were infected and fled also. However, once the information was passed that there were no tanks, the men returned to their stations.

At midnight, permission was granted to move the 23rd Division command post further to the rear, on the assumption that the situation on the Tali front had stabilized. This move was to prove an almost disastrous mistake, for the next morning, while the commanding officer and his staff were travelling to the new post, the front began to cave in. Only one staff officer remained at the old command post, and he could not reach his superior. When word finally reached the commander, between 9 and 10 that morning, he was too far from the action to direct the operations effectively. Consequently, the commanding officer of the 13th Infantry Regiment was placed in charge.

Confusion predominated for hours even with this change, since the 13th Infantry Regiment was quite far south of the breach. To complicate

matters further, the telephone wires had been cut, so contact between the various regimental and battalion command posts was broken. Nevertheless, preparations were begun for a counterattack to seal the gap. To this end, one company from the 13th Infantry Regiment was sent in haste to the threatened sector and a reserve battalion was put on alert.

By midday on the 9th, it was clear what had happened. A crack Russian company had crossed the flooding river, sometimes wading chest deep in the icy water, and had attacked immediately in spite of the extreme cold. Obviously, the counterattack had to get under way at the earliest possible moment, before the Russian company had time to obtain reinforcements and tanks. In the evening, the 23rd Division commander arrived and took charge, but by then his troops were already on the move. Within a short time, good news arrived: part of the area between Lakes Kärstilä and Leitimo had been retaken. Thus, in spite of the fact that Repola and Tali were in Russian hands, the front as a whole was stabilized.

However, the situation was still quite fluid and would obviously change quickly once the Russians got their tanks and artillery across the river. On the 10th, the Russians reached the south side of Lake Leitimo and on the 11th began an attack with tanks. Once again the Finnish line buckled, and there was little that could be done about it. By nightfall, the Russians had punched three holes in the Finnish lines around Lake Leitimo. The 23rd Division had used up its last reserves and now had to request reinforcements from I Army Corps, which was only able to send one weak battalion.

When the 12th dawned, the Finns found they had been pushed back about two and a half miles from their positions of 6th March. That day the whole sector enjoyed comparative quiet, as the Russians regrouped for the next phase of operations. But, just as elsewhere, when the Russians began the final thrust, which might have broken the Finnish lines permanently and opened the way for an invasion into the heartland, 11 am arrived, and both sides laid down their arms. Whether the Russians could have succeeded in making good a thrust from Tali westward through the Saimaa Lake system with its swamps flooded from the spring thaw will never be known. But it is certain that they would have had a most difficult time of it.

Meanwhile, at the far end of the defense line, from the railroad to the Vuoksi Waterway, I Army Corps was holding the front. It was at the hamlet of Vuosalmi that the major battle for this section developed. The terrain at Vuosalmi formed a natural defensive position. On the south-west shore of the Waterway ran a steep ridge which curved to the north-east, and it was on this high ground that the Finnish 23rd Infantry Regiment ensconced itself with its four artillery pieces, which arrived at the last minute before the battle. Behind them was the Waterway, frozen solid and about 100 yards wide at that point, with an island below the north-east end of the ridge. The island was also occupied by the Finns.

A lone outpost

The Finnish troops had hardly got themselves dug in on 29th February, when the enemy arrived on the scene and began an immediate attack. The first attack, which was primarily a reconnoitering expedition, was easily repulsed. But as the day waned, the Russians brought up tanks and artillery to soften up the Finnish positions on the ridge. In all of this action, the island did not escape the attention of the Russians, but the Finns cut lanes in the ice, which, even though they froze over almost immediately, did keep the tanks back for a time.

It was not until the 2nd that the enemy managed to make his first breach in the lines. This gap occurred in the area of the ferry, when about a battalion of enemy troops reached the shore. The Finnish soldiers trapped in the area called in their own artillery fire upon themselves and the enemy. When the smoke cleared, the Russians were gone, and the

Finns prepare for an attack against the Russian lines

Finnish troops emerged from their bunker unscathed.

On the 4th, the Russians made their first successful penetration, on the left of the Finnish line, and drove the Finns back to the island. A Finnish counterattack the next morning had finally to be called off, as the losses mounted. Another attack was made by a unit sent from the 8th Division, but this failed to move the enemy back. The only result was that the Finns were reduced to about 600 shells for their artillery, in the face of an approaching second enemy division.

The next day the Russians increased the pressure, concentrating for the most part on the island, until it was lost and the Finnish units withdrawn to the opposite shore. Although the Finns still held some positions on the south-west shore of the Waterway, they were tenuous at best. On the 6th, the Finns made a valiant effort to recapture the island but were driven back, with heavy losses. For the rest of the day, the Finnish positions across from the island were subjected to heavy bombardment;

the soldiers, without bunkers, could only hover in the snow, waiting for it to end.

An attempted crossing of the Waterway on the 7th was repulsed by a counterattack under cover of darkness. On the 8th, the Russians called in air strikes on the Finnish positions and supply lines in addition to a heavy artillery barrage. A new attack commenced after this softening-up operation, and by nightfall the enemy had made thirteen holes in the Finnish lines. Again, the Finns counterattacked but failed to dislodge the Russians. The first group of reinforcements from the 21st Division arrived shortly thereafter, and the exhausted front line troops were sent to the rear.

By 9th March, the Russians had three divisions drawn up against the Vuosalmi positions. That day saw another Russian penetration, which staggered the weary Finns; however, they soon regained their equilibrium and closed the breach. On the southwest shore, the remaining Finnish units somehow managed to withstand a massive Russian onslaught. All day on the 10th, the Russian artillery pounded the Finnish positions in preparation for an all-out general attack, which began on the 11th. This attack gained the Russians another half-mile, and another rupture in the Finnish lines appeared imminent. However, more reinforcements arrived in the evening, and the enemy thrust was stalled. That same day the last positions on the south-west shore were abandoned.

The battle raged with unabated fury throughout 12th March, with the line surging back and forth according to the fortunes of the opposing forces. By nightfall, the Finns were in such a bad position that serious consideration was given to the idea of withdrawing to an even less favorable position in the rear.

For the Finns at Vuosalmi, the 13th dawned to the sound and fury of an unrelenting cannonade, while

Lieutenant-General K L Oesch, commander of the newly-created Coast Group which was earmarked for the defense of the north shore of Viipuri Bay

bombers made sorties overhead. All telephone lines were cut, and no communications between the various command posts was possible, not even by courier, because of the intense artillery fire. Then, suddenly, the Russian guns fell silent, but no one among the Finns knew why. Finally, an infantry officer arrived and stated simply: 'Peace has been concluded.' So ended the battle of Vuosalmi.

Meanwhile, at Taipale, at the extreme eastern end of the Isthmus, the Russians made an eleventh-hour effort to break through Finnish resistance, but the war ended before they succeeded.

While II Army Corps held the Red Army at bay before the city, one of the fiercest struggles of the Winter War developed on the ice and islands in the Gulf of Finland at Viipuri Bay. In order to deal with the situation effectively, Mannerhiem put the troops defending the Gulf and Bay under a new command on 1st March. The new organization, called the

Finnish troops in one of the front-line bunkers

Coast Group, was placed under the experienced leadership of the Chief of the General Staff, Lieutenant-General K L Oesch. His troops consisted of the 4th Division and a number of independent battalions and batteries, the latter only partially trained and poorly equipped. In addition, there was a battalion from Lapland which had arrived in late February.

The winter of 1939-40 was one of the coldest on record, but up until February the weather had been the invaluable ally of the hard pressed Finns. Now, when spring should have helped them by breaking up the ice, winter held on to the advantage of the Russians. By this time, the ice was strong enough to bear the weight of tanks, and the lanes cut in the ice froze over almost immediately.

When the retreat to the rear positions was completed, two islands, Tuppura and Uuras, were still occupied by the Finns, although they were outside the new lines. These islands guarding the mouth of Viipuri Bay had been essential for the protection of the retreating forces. Once the rear positions were reached, the Finns found themselves with an additional eighteen miles to defend because of the ice on the bay, so the islands

continued to be important, especially in the face of the four divisions, along with their armored units, the enemy had massed south-west of Uuras.

Tuppura was attacked on 2nd March and lost after several assaults had been repulsed. After the first few failures, the Russians had developed a successful tactic for taking the island. They bombarded it from the ground and air and then surrounded it with tanks, thus cutting off the defenders from the mainland; the tanks then tightened the cordon and acted as a firing base on the ice, after which the infantry went in. This tactic was used throughout the Russian island-hopping operations. The next day, the Finnish garrison smashed its way through the ring of tanks and retreated to Säkkijärvi across the bay.

Although the loss of Tuppura was not serious, since it did not vitally affect the general situation, the loss of Teikari Island, which stands in front of Vilaniemi, was a matter of greater importance. It had not only protected the approaches to the north shore of the bay, but also those to the west flank of the forces holding Suonio Island – a keystone in the defense system of the bay. Two attempts to recapture the island on 2nd March failed. The loss of Teikari was to have serious consequences for

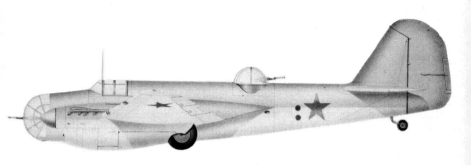

The Tupolev ANT-40 (SB-2bis). Companion of the DB-3 in the Winter War. The original version was used in the Spanish Civil War, and its experience in Spain led to the *bis* model, which had better engines and propellers, improved armament, and more sophisticated instrumentation and crew conditions. *Engines:* two M-103 inlines, 990-hp each. *Armament:* four 7.62mm machine guns and up to 1,430lbs of bombs. *Speed:* 280 mph at 16,400 feet. *Ceiling:* 27,900 feet. *Range:* 1,430 miles. *Weight empty/loaded:* 9,436/14,330 lbs. *Span:* 70 feet 6 inches. *Length:* 41 feet 6 inches. *Crew:* three.

the entire course of the battle for Viipuri. That same day the Russians used the island as a base for their landing on the north shore of Viipuri Bay at Vilaniemi and Häränpäänniemi.

A Finnish counterattack that night managed to throw the enemy back on the ice, but the following day he was back in force to re-establish his foothold and at the same time to drive toward Ristiniemi, at the mouth of the bay, where the heavy coastal batteries were located. Once again, the Russians were beaten back with the aid of reinforcements. According to reports from the defenders, the Russians had not used armored support on the 2nd and 3rd, which in large part accounted for their failure to procure a firm hold. Why they did not use tanks is a mystery, and one can only assume that they either feared to drive the tanks so far across the ice lest it give way or that the attack was intended only for reconnoitering. Thereafter the Red armored vehicles

were regular participants in all action on the north side of the bay and on the bay itself; moreover, their numbers increased with every passing day.

The presence of the tanks, however, was not as serious a problem to the defender as it might have been, because the light tanks most commonly employed by the Russians were not very efficient on the terrain where they had to operate. Because of the large granite outcroppings on the shore and the steep slopes leading up to the beaches, the tanks found it difficult to get off the ice. They had to seek out low and level points on the coast, and when they found them they frequently became stuck in the snow drifts. As time passed, however, the tank drivers learned from experience, becoming quite skilful and resourceful in adapting to the conditions on both the bay and the shore.

The common method of attacking the mainland used by the Russians was to select a point of land jutting out into the bay, draw their tanks up on both sides of it, and use them as a firing base to catch the defenders in a cross fire. Since these points were usually very rocky and had steep banks, the tanks would remain on the ice until the infantry had landed and then would head up the inlets to the end where there was usually a village and a road on which they could crawl up on land. Once this operation was completed, the tanks would spread out and cut off the defenders on the end of the point and also try to move into the interior.

By the 4th, the outer islands were abandoned in the face of overwhelming odds. Several courageous counterattacks on the 2nd and 3rd thinned the ranks of the units to such an extent that they had to be sent to the rear for rest and recuperation.

A general attack against all the Finnish positions commenced on the 4th. The enemy formations even came across the ice of the Gulf of Finland on this occasion, advancing from their bases on Suur, Lava, and Someri Islands toward Kotka and Hamina. These advances were checked by the coastal artillery, which wreaked havoc on the enemy columns as the exploding shells broke up the ice, drowning large numbers of men and causing panic among the survivors. These attacks did not affect the general situation, although they did arouse a great deal of concern in the Finnish High Command that the south coast would be occupied and the defenders at Viipuri outflanked. A battalion of young boys and men too old for military service was assembled and sent to the coast as reinforcements.

The cause of the greatest concern was the magnitude of the attacking force on Viipuri Bay, which imperiled the defenses of Viipuri. The Russians directed their heaviest fire at the upper end of the bay at Vilaniemi, launching an infantry regiment and a battalion of tanks against the de-

fenders. They soon had a foothold in the village; with an estimated two divisions pouring in behind them by nightfall, the situation along the sector Häränpäänniemi-Vilajoki-Vilaniemi was serious. During the night, however, the 9th Infantry Regiment from the 3rd Division was sent to bolster the buckling defenses.

Meanwhile, farther down the bay another Russian attack group was busy preparing to attack Suonio Island from Uuras Island, which had just been vacated. Enemy attacks at other points in the Bay had been repulsed with great difficulty. Until this time, the Coast Group had held its own, but it could not hope to continue doing so for much longer without more help. A request to II Army Corps commander stated the situation quite succinctly: all the reserves had been placed on the firing line, and the artillery batteries were in desperate need of shells. II Army Corps' commander was himself severely pressed. He had only 600 shells left in his stockpile, which had to suffice for the Coast Group and his own three divisions, all of which were also under constant attack.

Conflicting reports concerning the developments at Vilaniemi came in during the night. At first, it was reported that the Russians had been thrown back on the ice; then, that they were still holding positions on the mainland; later, that fourteen tanks had been captured at Vilajoki and finally that this was an incorrect report. In truth, at some points the enemy had been driven back on the ice, but by the morning of the 5th the Russians were firmly ensconsed on the north shore of the bay.

During the attacks of 5th March, the Russians assaulted all the island positions right up to Kulp Island, immediately in front of Viipuri. The Finns sawed lanes in the ice in front of the island at other points, but they immediately froze solid, and the tanks drove across them with impunity. The attacking infantry

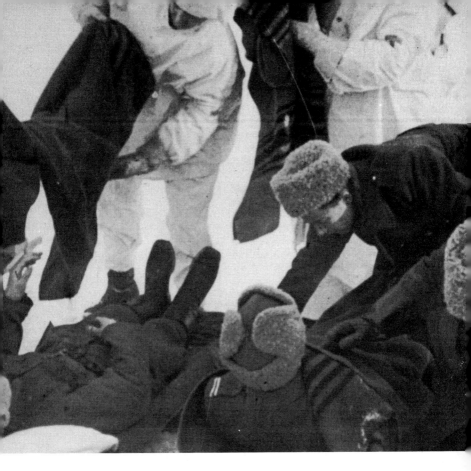

used the piles of ice blocks as cover to fire on the defenders.

By this time, the enemy was attacking the bay area with three of the four divisions there, and sixteen divisions were operating against the whole Viipuri front from the bay to Vuoksi, while another ten divisions operated from there to Lake Ladoga. The Finns had the Coast Group and six divisions on the Viipuri front as far as Vuosalmi, but their reserve forces were almost entirely deployed, while munitions and supplies were dangerously low. On the other hand, the Russians had an effectively unlimited source of supplies and men. Even getting supplies where they were needed became a cause of growing concern for the Finnish commanders. In the early stages of the battle for Viipuri,

Casualties continue to mount

the road system on the north side of the bay was used to supply the Coast Group from the supply depots of II Army Corps, but as the battle increased in violence the roads were choked with refugees and supply traffic. The problems were compounded by the air raids. When the Russians gained a foothold on the north shore of the bay, the supply situation became almost impossible to deal with.

In spite of these difficulties, the Finns had no choice but to fight on, and the Russians did not ease the pressure. They had the initiative, they used it to the fullest advantage. On the 6th, the Soviet troops took part of the village of Nisolahti, while another group breached the lines at Niskapohja. By midday, they had established a beachhead on the point between Turki Island and Majapohja, and shortly thereafter they seized a position on the south-west side of Majapohja. By nightfall, the circumstances were such that the commander of the 4th Division considered pulling his east wing back so far that it would have exposed the right wing of the 3rd Division, which was quite weak already, since its reserves had been transferred to Vilaniemi. The commander also requested reinforcements to hold Neula Island, where he feared a major breakthrough. But all that could be spared for the defense of Neula Island was part of a reserve regiment from the 5th Division.

Quite clearly, the island front was approaching a crisis, and it was equally obvious that little material or human help was available to stem the tide. It was only a question of time before the whole island defense system crumbled and the troops would be forced to withdraw to the north shore. When this happened, the entire west wing of II Army Corps and the supply lines running northwest around Viipuri would be jeopardized.

Throughout 7th March, the merciless Russian juggernaut pushed forward, while its artillery and airplanes pounded the Finnish positions and supply lines. The Viipuri-Hamina road was cut at Vilaniemi, making it necessary for whatever reinforcements the Finns could send to any threatened point to skirt the lines. By the same evening, it was evident that the island defenses from Suonio Island to Majapohja were untenable, and the men were withdrawn the next day after savage battles.

One by one, the islands had been abandoned, and for the most part the Finns were fighting on the mainland, except for Piispa Island, where a

Even bicycles are withdrawn to deny their use to the Russians

small force was still holding out. Between Vilaniemi and Nisalahti, no changes of any significance had occurred inspite of the fierceness of the struggle.

An even more massive attack began on the 9th. Finnish air reconnaissance reported that a seven-mile column of Russian troops and tanks was crossing the ice between Pullinniemi and Vilaniemi, heading north-west. This meant that a whole division of fresh troops was to be hurled into the battle on the Viipuri-Hamina road behind Vilaniemi, where it was estimated that two divisions were already in action.

At the same time, the commander of the Finnish 4th Division was growing anxious about his exposed troops on Piispa Island, since he feared a breach in his lines on the mainland. Even with the reinforce-

The retreat continues

ments he had received earlier, he did not believe he could hold his positions. That evening the island was abandoned, and the men moved to Koivuniemi. This move allowed the Russians to make a breach in the lines between the forces of the Coast Group and II Army Corps. The 14th Infantry Regiment, reinforced by a weak battalion from the 3rd Division, had to be sent in to seal the gap before the rear positions were completely enveloped.

The next day, the Russians attempted to roll up the Finnish defenses on the point at Majapohja and simultaneously attacked Porkka Island, the only island still remaining in Finnish hands. In spite of their exhaustion, the troops of the 4th Division initiated a counterattack which was at first successful but was finally repulsed. By that night, the Russians were in possession of both places.

While the battle was raging further

up the bay, at Vilaniemi the Russians were using their fresh troops to good advantage. Wherever they created a hole in the line, the Russians quickly pushed on beyond the highway, thus giving themselves a deepened and extended front. But even with new troops and their deepened position, however, the Russians were unable to push the Finns back east or west, as would have been expected.

For all their material superiority, the Russians were moving more slowly than they had anticipated. After ten days, they had only reached the north shore of the bay and were experiencing difficulties in their attempt to roll up the Finnish defenses from the rear. However, the situation was verging on disaster for the Finns, should any one point give way completely. Whatever the disaster staring them in the face, the Finns held out, and the Russian drive to reach Viipuri from the north shore was halted.

On the 11th, the enemy again made a push which was stoutly resisted. Again on the 12th, they tried to break through the area between the 4th Division and II Army Corps, causing the defenders to pull back to the area between Ahokas and Rasalahti. On the 13th, the Russians continued to attack right up to the moment when the ceasefire went into effect. Apparently, they hoped to break through and move on to capture Viipuri.

When the guns fell silent, the Russians held only part of Viipuri, and that could never be considered a victory for Stalin's army. The Finns had acquitted themselves with valor, and it is beyond question that their's was the moral victory. But they had had no real hope of getting the trained manpower to hold the lines. Even if they had received enough materials and supplies to carry on, they would have been crushed in a matter of weeks.

The watching giants

No account of the Winter War would be complete without some comments about its international significance. When Russia hurled herself upon Finland, Europe was already technically at war. In many ways the future role of the Soviet Union in the Second World War was determined by the events of her three-month war with Finland. The liquidation of Poland had given the world a hint of the efficiency of the Nazi war machine, but thus far nothing had occurred to reveal Russia's military ability. By all the usual criteria, the Soviet Union was reckoned a great power, but until December, 1939, there was no adequate measure by which to gauge her military effectiveness. Thus it was with acute interest that the other great powers watched the unfolding of the drama played out under the northern lights.

Although probably no country watched the stumbling giant with greater interest and more analytically than Germany, she was bound to neutrality by treaty, and she loyally observed her obligations. Every request by the Finnish Government for aid, diplomatic or material, was rejected by the Reich. Germany even went so far as to stop the shipment to

The strength of the Nazi war machine is revealed as Hitler sends his troops into Poland in September, 1939. At this date Russia remained an unknown quantity

Winston Churchill encouraged the British Admiralty to consider plans for severing Germany's iron ore supplies from Sweden

Finland of Italian airplanes that had arrived at a north German port.

More germane to the subject are the attitudes and views of Britain and France, the only other two states powerful enough to render any significant help to the Finns. Both countries were at war with Germany, and both saw in the Russo-Finnish conflict multiple possibilities: alleviation of pressure on the French front by opening a new theater of operations against Germany in the North; cutting off vital iron ore shipments from Sweden to Germany; striking a blow against Bolshevism; fulfilling the moral obligations in large part neglected since 1919. Consequently, the Allies took more than a passing interest in Finland's plight, but they did not commit themselves immediately. They had to wait and see if Finland would survive the initial onslaught before they seriously considered rendering any substantial aid.

Allied military interest in Scandinavia was not, of course, a recent development. During the First World War, the British had mined Norwegian waters, and they were considering doing so again. Moreover, the British Admiralty, prodded by Winston Churchill, had, in September 1939, already begun to prepare a plan to force passage into the Baltic Sea in order to cut Germany off from her Swedish iron ore supplies. The League of Nations' resolution calling on all nations to aid Finland provided the legal rationale, while the success of Finnish arms gave practical grounds, for implementing open Allied intervention in Scandinavia. Ostensibly, the intervention would be directed against Russia, but who could blame the Allies if an open confrontation developed with Germany in the process? Of course, in the initial stages, the Scandinavian states were not asked whether they were amenable to providing a battleground for the great powers.

For its part, the Finnish Government was ready and eager to accept

French Premier Daladier visits a defense exposition in 1939

offers of aid from anywhere, however it might discomfort her neighbors. Finland's remoteness, however, made her dependent upon the Scandinavian states, particularly Sweden, for a great part of her war materials and food supplies, as well as on the good will of Sweden and Norway, if any substantial numbers of troops from the Allies were to reach the Finnish front.

It is in this context that the Allied offers of aid must be evaluated. Unquestionably, the idea of sending troops to Finland inspired more enthusiasm in the French that in the British Government. When the question was first raised in the Allied Supreme Council on 19th December, 1939, Premier Daladier of France expressed his desire to dispatch an expeditionary force to Finland immediately. For their part, the British took a more cautious approach, wanting to avoid an open breach with the Soviet Union before they had taken stock of all the facts. It was finally agreed to aid Finland indirectly at first with technicians and sup-

plies and to take up the matter of transit through Norway and Sweden with their respective governments.

The question of transit rights was broached with the Norwegian and Swedish governments on 27th December; on 4th January 1940, the two governments gave a favorable response, but with the proviso that the supplies be shipped under the guise of Finnish purchases abroad. A few days later Finland was permitted to begin recruiting volunteers in the United Kingdom, and the British Government undertook to secure transit rights across Scandinavia for the volunteer units. Neither Norway or Sweden objected to this traffic.

Meanwhile, the question of official Allied intervention in the conflict was still hanging fire. Several plans were given serious consideration, among them one which would have directed an attack upon the Russians via Petsamo. For this purpose, three Polish destroyers and two submarines which had been incorporated into the British navy were to sail to Petsamo to blockade the port and simultaneously to cut off the Russian divisions operating in the Arctic. General Sikorski, head of the Polish Government in Exile, approved the plan, but the British vetoed it because Petsamo's isolated position and the difficulties of transportation from there to the main theater of war made it impractical. The French proposed to plan for an attack through Turkey and the Black Sea, which would have caused the Russians to transfer large numbers of troops to the south to protect the oil-rich Caucasus but this plan, too, was discarded.

That the Allies even seriously considered these plans indicates the secondary importance they attached to the Finnish war itself. Their main interest was to open a second front, and each of the plans might have done that – at the expense of Finland – but the points of invasion were too far removed from the Continent to affect the German war effort

General Sikorski's Government-in-Exile sanctioned the scheme to use Polish warships to blockade Petsamo. Britain eventually vetoed the plan immediately. What was needed was a plan which posed a more direct threat to Germany in order to make her shift large numbers of divisions from the French frontier at once. For this purpose, the most feasible area was the Scandinavian Peninsular – in particular, Narvik and the railroad from there to Lulea. A move there would serve a threefold purpose: firstly, Narvik, the winter port for shipping iron ore to Germany, would thus be effectively closed to German use; secondly, the railroad, which passed through the Swedish iron ore fields, could be prevented from shipping any more ore to Germany through the Baltic Sea; thirdly, with its connections to Finland, the railroad would be the quickest and easiest means to get troops to the Finnish front. The first two steps were calculated to open the second front against Germany, and, as all later operational plans were to indicate, this goal remained uppermost in the minds of the Allied strategists.

Although the final decision to occupy Narvik was not made until 5th February, contingency plans for the measure were already prepared in December. The final plans were more ambitious, however, clearly indicating the Allies' wider purpose in calling for the occupation not only of Narvik, but also of Trondheim, Bergen, and Stavanger, and the training of troops for operations to forestall German military intervention in Sweden.

All the planning and problems attendant upon an Allied expedition were recognized by the Finns, who knew in reality that there was little hope of help arriving in time or in sufficient force to change the course of the war. But they also recognized the very real psychological value of such preparations in bringing the Russians to the negotiating table. Moreover, the proposals could be calculated to evoke more action and obtain more support from Norway and Sweden on Finland's behalf.

Consequently, as the February offensive gained momentum on the Isthmus, the Finnish government undertook a twofold policy. On the one hand, it sought to establish contact with the Kremlin, via Stockholm, with the aim of ending the war. On the other, it pursued the Allied offers of assistance. The threat of Allied intervention was used in an effort to temper the Russian peace terms and, hopefully, to get Germany to put pressure on Moscow to end the war. The possibility of peace was employed to gain larger troop commitments from the Allies.

When the Allied plan to come to Finland's aid was first announced in early February, the proposal was so vague that not even an anticipated departure date could be given. At this time, London and Paris indicated they were prepared to forego diplomatic niceties and just let the troop transports appear at Narvik without prior consultation with Oslo and Stockholm.

By 27th February, the Allied proposal was somewhat more specific; at least a date – 15th March – was given for the departure of the troop transports, with an anticipated arrival date in Finland of 15th April. The numbers of troops and the amount of supplies and weapons had not as yet been spelled out, however. Mannerheim had the impression that the number of men expected to reach Finland would be quite small, since most of the contingent would be left in Norway and Sweden on garrison duty. Contrary to earlier statements, the Finns were now told they would have to secure the necessary transit rights for the troops from Oslo and Stockholm. When the two governments were approached on the question a couple of days later, they rejected the suggestion out of hand,, even as they had denied all previous requests for active intervention in the war or for permission to transport anything but volunteers across their territories.

Indirect peace talks had meanwhile

been initiated between Helsinki and Moscow; in these talks, the Russians had made it clear that their territorial demands were now much larger than they had been the previous autumn. The Kremlin now wanted the entire Karelian Isthmus and a thirty-year lease of Hanko Cape as a naval base; moreover, it was intimated that the demands would increase if the Finns did not accept the terms immediately.

When word leaked out that peace feelers were being made toward Moscow, the Allies made more positive proposals. Peace would have been disadvantageous to the Allies, since it would have meant the end of the disruption of Russia's economy and the fulfilment of her commercial obligations to Germany. On the 28th, the British Minister to Helsinki, Gordon Vereker, informed the Finnish Government that the British were prepared to dispatch some 13,000 men by mid-April in addition to the troops to remain in Norway and Sweden. Details concerning the execution of the plan and the kinds of forces involved were not spelled out, but the Finns were assured that the troops would remain in Finland until a final peace settlement.

On the 29th, when it became known that definite steps to end the war were in progress and that Mannerheim had categorically advised his government to make peace immediately, a new offer was made by the Allies. Charles Magny, the French Minister in Helsinki, asserted that an Anglo-French force of 20,000 men was prepared to leave at once for Finland. He urged the Finns to continue the war and warned that if they did not, Finland would have to assume full responsibility for whatever territorial amputations and economic losses she might incur as the result of a peace treaty. Magny's information and assertions

Danish volunteers were among the few foreign nationals who actually saw service in Finland after the appeal by the League of Nations

Charles Magny, the French Minister in Helsinki. He gave promises of Anglo-French aid

convinced the Finns that the Allies were more interested in opening a second front against Germany than in really aiding Finland and that the Allies were not coordinating their policy, since there was such disparity between the British and French proposals. Hence, it was decided to make peace at the earliest possible moment.

That night, the Finnish Minister in Paris, Harri Holma, reported that Daladier had promised to send 50,000 troops to Finland, that they would depart by 12th March, and that the Allies would solve the problem of transit rights through Scandinavia. But this promise was subject to approval in London. A prerequisite of this aid, moreover, was that Helsinki break off all negotiations with Moscow, otherwise the whole project would be dropped.

The French offer was tempting, but it also placed the Finnish government on the horns of a cruel dilemma: whether to make peace with the

Russians on less than favorable terms, but at least to save what was left of the country, or to wait for Allied aid in the hope that the spring thaw would arrive quickly and thus stem the Russian advance long enough for the Allies to reach Finland. The Finnish Government decided to request further clarification of the latest Soviet terms and at the same time to ascertain the expected arrival date of the Anglo-French force. The Finns also asked the Allies to send a hundred bombers with arms and crews at once.

The next few days were chaotic; the only two certainties which emerged from the confusion were that the Finnish Army was near total ex-

Helsinki receives the services of British firemen

haustion and that the Allies could not settle between themselves the exact size of the proposed force or how transit rights were to be arranged in the face of Swedish and Norwegian objections. The Swedish Prime Minister had warned Tanner that if the Allies attempted to force passage to Finland, the Swedes would find themselves in the war on the side of Russia. On 2nd March, the Allies promised the bombers at once and declared that the expedition would sail on 15th March. The next day Vereker said only 6,000 British troops would be sent, but they would leave on the 11th, if Finland made an official request by the 5th. On the 6th, the French informed the Finns that an initial force of 18,000 Frenchmen and 12,000 Britons would embark in a week's time, accompanied

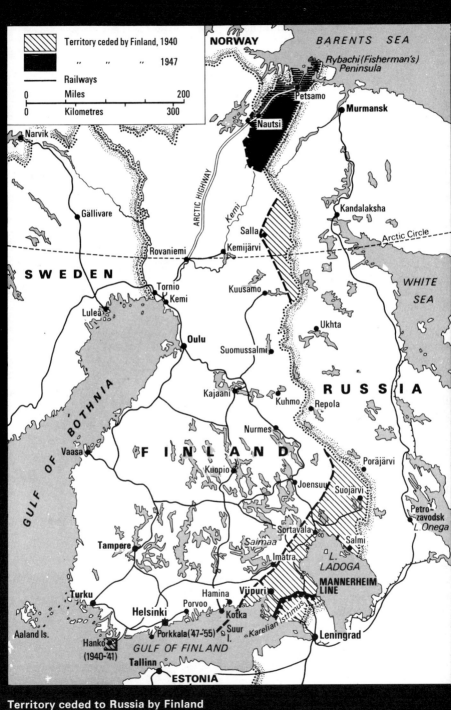

Territory ceded to Russia by Finland

by seventy-two bombers. Even if these forces were attacked by the Germans, the number of troops destined for Finland would not be diminished. Moreover, the French were assured that Sweden would not oppose the transit of the troops.

The growing disparity between the ambitious French plans and the more modest British proposals gave the Finns cause for further discussion. Upon due consideration, they decided peace was the only solution and sent a delegation to Moscow to negotiate. This resolve was the only rational one to be made under the circumstances, since the nation was threatened by total disaster if the army collapsed, for the Russian demands would increase in proportion to the success of the Red Armies. However, the Finns did not close the door entirely on the Allies; they asked for an extension of the deadline until the 12th for a request of aid.

Anglo-French attempts to keep the Finns fighting were continued until the very end. On the 7th, the Allies promised to dispatch 15,500 men to Narvik on 15th March, and these troops were to be followed by 42,000 more as soon as rail transportation permitted. Then, on the 8th, Daladier sent a communiqué urging the Finnish Government to accept the Anglo-French offer or assume full responsibility for the consequences of making peace with Russia. This statement, akin Magny's earlier remark, reveals as much of the Frenchman's lack of understanding and of sympathy with Finland in her agony and danger as it does of his desire to establish a second front against Germany. There can be little doubt that any Allied aid would have been too little and too late to save Finland, and this certainly should have been realized in Paris.

In spite of the enormity of the

Finnish representatives under a flag of truce prepare to cross the front line to negotiate peace terms with the Russians

Soviet demands the Finns decided to sign the treaty. What the Russians now demanded and received was about ten per cent of Finland's territory – all of the Karelian Isthmus, including Viipuri, the territory north of Lake Ladoga, which included the communes of Sortavala and Kuusamo, and the Finnish islands in the eastern end of the Gulf of Finland, including Suur Island. Finland also agreed to lease Hanko Cape to the Soviet Union as a naval base for thirty years, to build a railroad from Salla to Kemijärvi, and to sign a defense pact with the Russians. As a result of the territorial amputations, Finland lost about twelve per cent of her economic base and also had to relocate the people of the ceded territories, most of whom chose to move inside the new frontiers rather than live under Soviet rule. The total number of people to be resettled was about 450,000 or approximately ten per cent of the Finnish population.

For Finland, the ordeal of war was over. To her undying credit, what she had done, she had done alone, virtually unaided. In retrospect, the Allied offers of aid appear chimerical after the events of May and June 1940. Still,

Above: **The peace delegation crosses the demarcation line during the peace talks.** *Right:* **Finnish civilians receive news of the capitulation**

the Finns cannot be faulted for using the offer of aid as best they could to keep the Russians from occupying the whole country. Though there is little evidence to prove it, there can be small doubt that the Anglo-French interest in the conflict influenced the Kremlin to make peace. In spite of the fact that the Soviet Union was allied with Germany at the time, Stalin in all likelihood did not wish an open rupture with the West, and as events proved, he made a wise decision.

For the Scandinavian states, especially Sweden, the end of the war was a welcome relief. In international politics, the sovereignty and independent action of small states is all too frequently abridged and circumscribed by the national and international interests of their great neighbors. Such was the case with Sweden. Under pressure at home and abroad, the Swedish Government had been in an increasingly uncomfortable position for the preceding three months. On

the one hand, the immense popularity and support of the Finnish cause in Sweden, originating in the ancient cultural and historical associations between the two states, as well as the natural human tendency to side with the underdog, had placed the Swedish Government in an embarrassing and, perhaps, ultimately untenable political position, especially when the Allies requested transit rights to Finland for their troops. On the other hand, the subtle and not so subtle diplomatic coercion and duress to which Sweden was subjected by the Soviet Union and Germany militated against active and overt support of Finland. Moral questions aside, Sweden pursued a course best calculated to preserve her own independence, and by doing so, she was able to send material aid to Finland after the war.

What it meant

Any analysis of the impact of the Winter War on later development must begin with a consideration of how Germany evaluated the war, for, as the storm center of Europe, her actions and attitudes in large part determined the future course of events. Hitler and his military leaders were hardly displeased by the reverses of the Red Army and, if anything, the Winter War enhanced their sense of Germanic superiority over the Slav. But their conviction of superiority also blinded them to the realities of what the experience meant to the Soviet military command and what influence it had upon the reorganization, training, and equipping of Russian troops. Hitler's underestimation of Soviet military potential and his decision to invade Russia before defeating Britain were in part the result of the Winter War.

If one reviews only the statistics of Russian losses of men and material, it becomes clear why Hitler believed the Soviet Union was a bumbling giant incapable of resisting the German war machine. By the time the war ended, the Red forces massed against Finland totalled forty-five divisions; if one includes the special units and rear echelons, the forces amounted to approximately a million men. Of these it is conservatively estimated, at least 200,000 were killed and an unknown number wounded. In contrast, Finnish casualties were 68,480, of which 24,923 were killed or missing and

The cost of sub-zero warfare: the frozen corpse of a Russian lieutenant

43,557 wounded. The poor showing of Russian armored forces and severe losses suffered by these units would have convinced anyone of the incompetency of the Soviet military. Against the Finns, the Russians had ranged 3,200 tanks, light, medium and heavy, and of these the Finns captured or destroyed 1,600, not to mention the 3,000 to 4,000 trained specialists who perished or were captured. The Red Air Force did no better, having lost over 900 planes in the war.

But the figures do not reveal the causes for the Soviet losses or what the Russians later did to eliminate them. The Soviet army, expecting to fight a conventional war with Finland, had entered combat with an army trained to fight in a very different kind of geographic and environmental setting. It was not prepared for the sub-arctic weather and had not analyzed the topography or the sort of defenses the army would come up against, although the Intelligence division must have had information concerning these matters. The 163rd Ukrainian Division, for example, was plucked directly from the plains and sent to Suomussalmi without being re-equipped or retrained for the type of warfare that was ahead. It would have been a simple matter to have given these men training in forest combat in the Moscow military district or in Russian Karelia, especially since the invasion was planned at least a few months before it occurred.

Operating on conventional military strategy, the Russians were no match for the Finnish guerrilla tactics; time after time, especially in the early stages of the war, they proved themselves incapable of imaginative innovations in the face of the unusual. Even on the Karelian Isthmus, when they forced the Finns to retreat, the Red Army commanders did not exhibit any great ability to follow up an initial success; thus, the Finns were able to withdraw safely every time. This lack of imagination was one of the basic reasons for the terrible losses suffered by the Soviet forces.

However, what the German military failed to take into consideration, or failed to notice, about the Russians in the Winter War was their ability to dig in and build bunkers that could withstand all but a direct hit, as well as their expertise in house-to-house fighting in the villages. At Stalingrad, these abilities were to stand the Russians in good stead. Another factor in the war which the Germans did not take into account was the unfamiliar environment in which the Russians were fighting. When Germany attacked Russia, the Soviet soldiers fought in familiar surroundings, and they fought for their homes. If at first the Red Armies reeled before the Nazi onslaught, their stand at Stalingrad redeemed them. Finally, the Nazis were unaware that the political commissars attached to every unit of the Red Army had a debilitating effect on the decision-making of the military commanders. This dual system of command seriously affected the efficiency of the army, but, apparently as a result of the war, the system was abolished in August, 1940. Thus, the military commanders had an opportunity to reorganize the armed services without the sort of political interference they had suffered earlier. After Hitler's invasion in 1941, political commissars were once again placed with every unit, but in 1943 their influence was curtailed, though not abolished altogether.

As a result of the war, the Russian armed forces, under the leadership of Marshal Timoshenko, underwent a root and branch reorganization. The rank of general and other ranks were reintroduced, with most of the privileges attached to them. Greater emphasis was placed on training and

Above: A Russian tank captured by the Finns. The numerical supremacy but poor handling of Russian armor was constant throughout the conflict.
Below: Finnish prisoners return home after the surrender

The Russian's skill in bunker construction during the Winter War passed unnoticed by the Germans with terrible results when they themselves attacked Stalingrad

proper equipment. Although the reorganization was not completed by the time Hitler ordered his armies to march, the Red Army was in better form than it would have been without the experience of the Winter War. Timoshenko remarked to the Finnish Military Attaché on one occasion that the Russians had learned a good deal in the war with Finland.

Although it is unlikely that Hitler ever intended to honor the treaty with Russia for its full term, the Winter War apparently determined him to move against the Soviet Union at the earliest possible moment. In July, 1940, he ordered the preparation of plans for the invasion, and by December, the plan was well on its way towards final form. During September, the Finns and the Germans entered into an agreement permitting German troops to travel through Finland to and from the German bases in northern Norway. In December, General Heinrichs of Mannerheim's staff lectured the German military staff on the techniques of Arctic warfare. When the invasion of Russia began in June 1941, the Finns, although never officially or formally allied with the Reich, joined in the fight to regain their lost territories. They recaptured them only to lose them again at the end of the Second World War.

The Winter War also turned Germany's interest towards Norway. As a result of the Allied plans to transport troops across Norwegian territory to

Above: **General Heinrichs and Marshal Mannerheim. The former lectured the OKW on the principles of arctic warfare prior to Operation Barbarossa. *Right:* Finland's troops were numerically inferior, yet their doggedness and ability drove them to inflict humiliatingly disproportionate losses on the Russians**

Finland, Hitler decided that Norway had to be occupied as soon as possible. Already in December, 1939, Hitler had spoken with Vidkun Quisling, a Norwegian Nazi, about establishing a Nazi régime in Norway. The Allies, of course, had not lost their interest in Norway either after the Finns capitulated. The plan to mine the Norwegian coastal waters was still in effect, and on the day of the Nazi occupation the British ships had sailed towards Norway for that purpose.

Finally, and most generally, one must not overlook the psychological and moral effect of the Winter War on the Allied war effort. In a climate of international lawlessness, the Finns had been forced to resort to arms to protect their liberty. Their splendid courage and daring in the face of hopeless odds set an example for the entire world. Though the cost was high, the Finns had been willing to pay the price to save their freedom. That the Finns lost the war fades into insignificance when it is recalled that she emerged with her right to freedom vindicated.

Bibliography

Memoirs, C G Mannerhiem (Cassell and Co, London)

The Diplomacy of the Winter War, Max Jakobsen (Harvard University Press, Cambridge, Mass; London University Press, London)

Finland and World War II, 1939-1944, John Wuorinen, ed (The Ronald Press, New York)

The Winter War, V Tanner (Stanford University Press, Stanford)

Finland between East and West, A Mazour (D Van Nostrand Co, Inc, Princeton, NJ)

Finland in the Second World War, L Lundin (University of Indiana Press, Bloomington, Indiana)

Gesandter Zwischen Diktatur und Demokratie, Wipert von Bluecher (Wiesbaden)

So Kaempfte Finnland: Der Finnische-Sowjetische Krieg, 1939-40, J O Hannula (Wiking Verlag, Berlin)